Seaside Home

25 Stitched Projects from Sea Creatures to Sailboats

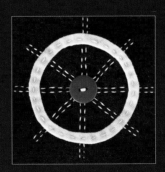

Compiled by Susanne Woods

stash BOOKS ®

an imprint of C&T Publishing

Publisher: Amy Marson

Creative Director: Gailen Runge

Acquisitions Editor: Susanne Woods

Editor: Cynthia Bix

Technical Editors: Teresa Stroin and
Priscilla Read

Cover/Book Designer: Kristy Zacharias

Production Coordinator: Jenny Davis

Production Editor: S. Michele Fry

Illustrator: Kirstie L. Pettersen

Photography by Christina Carty-Francis
and Diane Pedersen of C&T Publishing,
Inc., unless otherwise noted

Published by Stash Books, an imprint of C&T Publishing, Inc., P.O. Box 1456, Lafayette, CA 94549

Library of Congress Cataloging-in-Publication Data

Seaside home : 25 stitched projects from sea creatures to sailboats / compiled by Susanne Woods.

   p. cm.

 ISBN 978-1-60705-414-6

1. Embroidery. 2. Quilting. 3. Fancy work. I. Woods, Susanne.

 TT770.S43 2012

 746.44--dc23

                              2011027650

Contents

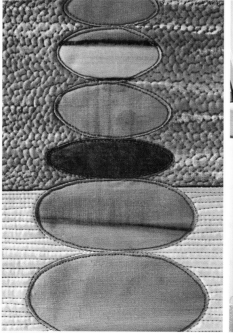

Introduction

Oh! I do like to be beside the seaside!

I do like to be beside the sea!

I do like to stroll upon the Prom, Prom, Prom!
Where the brass bands play: "Tiddely-om-pom-pom!"

So just let me be beside the seaside
I'll be beside myself with glee

—John A. Glover-Kind, 1907

Who doesn't like to be beside the seaside? The sound of the seagulls, the relaxed readers in lounge chairs wearing inappropriately high knee socks, the children screeching with delight as each wave rolls in, and the intoxicating perfume of sunblock mixed with salty air and heat that only ever occurs at the sea…bliss. For me, I am happiest at the sea, and the inspiration to capture in craft the easy calm I feel there is unavoidably alluring.

In compiling this fifth book within our best-selling series of Design Collective titles, I have come to the slightly unnerving realization that many of the ideas behind these previous titles began with my frustration; I was not able to find exactly what I wanted, made with the quality I like. This book, I am thrilled to say, saw its beginnings from a much happier place—the love, the joy, the universal draw of the seaside!

As the acquisitions editor for Stash Books, I have invited a group of incredibly talented designers to share their fabulous creations that were inspired by their love of the sea. Each of these unique projects can be used, displayed, or worn to help bring a little bit of the seaside into your every day. Within these pages you will find quilts, softies, embroideries, bunting, and even a sunhat and beach bag. Some of the projects are easily achievable, and some are a bit more challenging, but all are artful, original, and charming designs that I hope you enjoy making for and gifting to yourself, friends, and family.

Beach Hut Pillow

FINISHED PILLOW SIZE: 15″ × 15″

In the United Kingdom, a day at the beach wouldn't be the same without brightly colored beach huts dotting the sand—tiny havens for changing into swim gear before heading out into the waves. Capture some of their charm with this cheery appliquéd pillow.

ARTIST: Jenny Arnott

WEBSITES: jennyarnott.co.uk
jennyarnott.blogspot.com

Jenny Arnott is a designer-maker producing embroidered textiles and accessories. Working from her UK studio, she carefully makes everything by hand using a combination of machine embroidery and appliqué. A lover of fabric, Jenny has an ever-growing collection of colorful and interesting materials to work with, including lots of pretty floral prints, ginghams, stripes, and polka dots. Her work includes little embroidered badges, buttons, handbag mirrors, lavender bags, and cushions.

Materials and Supplies

- Pale blue fabric: 1 fat quarter for pillow front
- Natural-colored fabric: ½ yard for pillow back
- Assorted scraps of plain and patterned red, blue, white, and beige fabrics for appliqué
- Contrasting thread
- Permanent marking pen (optional)
- 16″ square pillow form

Cutting

PALE BLUE FABRIC

Cut 1 square 15½″ × 15½″.

NATURAL-COLORED FABRIC

Cut 1 rectangle 15½″ × 10½″.

Cut 1 rectangle 15½″ × 11½″.

Instructions

Note: All seam allowances are ¼".

RAW-EDGE APPLIQUÉ

1. Trace the patterns (page 9) and make the templates for the hut and bunting flag pieces. Place them on the back of the assorted fabric scraps and cut out the number indicated on the patterns.

2. Position the beach hut on the pillow front panel near the bottom right corner. Using contrasting thread, stitch the hut in place using 2 lines of stitching for emphasis and leaving the edges raw. Stitch the door, doorframe, doorstep, door plaque, beach hut roof, and life ring in the same manner.

3. Position and stitch the bunting flags at regular intervals. Add the bunting ribbon by sewing a continuous line between flags. Go over the stitch line 2 or 3 times for emphasis.

To the right of the beach hut, continue the stitch line to the edge of the fabric. On the left, finish it toward the bottom left corner, in line with the base of the beach hut.

4. Stitch a small peg at the end of the bunting ribbon and stitch a number onto the beach hut door. Another option is to draw the bunting ribbon, small peg, and number using a permanent fine-tipped fabric marker.

PILLOW ASSEMBLY

1. Turn under a long edge ¼" to the wrong side on each pillow back piece. Turn under a second ¼" and press. Pin and machine stitch to create a neat edge.

2. Place the larger piece wrong side up with the turned-under edge toward the top. Place the second piece wrong side up on top of the first piece, with the turned-under edge toward the bottom. Overlap the pieces to form a square measuring 15½" × 15½".

3. Where the 2 pieces overlap, baste together securely by hand at each side.

4. Place the front and back panels right sides together, matching the edges. Pin and baste.

5. Sew around the edge completely, using a ¼″ seam allowance. Reinforce the stitching using either an overlock or a zigzag stitch, paying special attention to the corners. Remove all basting.

6. Trim any loose threads, trim the corners, and turn the pillow cover right side out. Press.

7. Insert the pillow form.

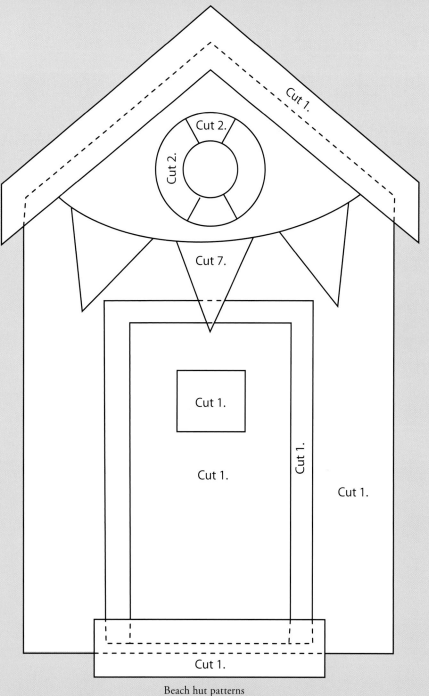

Cut 1.

Cut 2.

Cut 2.

Cut 7.

Cut 1.

Cut 1.

Cut 1.

Cut 1.

Cut 1.

Beach hut patterns

Coquillages à la Plage:
A Seaside Garland

FINISHED GARLAND LENGTH:
About 2 yards

These lovely white coquillages *(seashells) might have washed up on a romantic dream beach* (la plage). *Strung in a simple garland along with messages—perhaps found in fine old wine bottles?— they lend a bit of Gallic panache to your home.*

ARTIST: Janine Chani Attia

WEBSITES: blancetcaramel.com
blancetcaramel.etsy.com

Janine Chani Attia's work is influenced by her everyday life in romantic Paris. In its flea markets, she finds both inspiration and unique treasures for crafting projects. A dream came true when in 2010 she opened her Etsy shop, *Blanc et Caramel* (white and caramel—the colors she uses in her work). Finally she could share a bit of her Paris world with people from far away. In her shop she offers a wide range of handmade products: decorations such as scented sachets and garlands, jewelry made with flea market finds, even stamped note cards, tags, and much more. Be inspired and enjoy. *Bisous* (kisses)!

Materials and Supplies

- White muslin: ⅛ yard
- Thick, textured white or off-white cotton fabric: 1 fat quarter
- Natural-colored linen: 1 fat quarter
- Mother-of-pearl buttons (vintage or new): 6
- Twine: approximately 2 yards
- Cream-colored raffia: A few strings
- Rubber stamp with a compass motif (or motif of your choice)
- Alphabet rubber stamps
- Black ink pad for fabric
- Fabric glue
- Instant coffee to dye muslin

Cutting

WHITE MUSLIN

Tear off 2 strips ⅞″ × width of fabric; cut each in quarters to make 8 strips, each 10″ long.

Instructions

SEASHELLS

1. Trace the patterns (page 112) and cut out templates for the scallop, starfish, and conch. Cut 2 of each shape from the textured white cotton.

2. Pin the fabric shapes, right sides up, to the linen; use scissors to cut out the linen around the shapes, leaving a margin of about ⅜".

3. Machine stitch the seashell shapes to the linen with white thread, about ⅛" from the raw edges.

4. Mark decorative stitching lines as shown on the patterns and machine stitch. Sew 3 buttons on each starfish as shown.

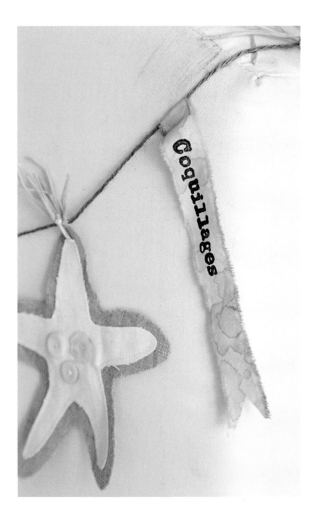

COFFEE-STAINED FLAGS

You need 7 strips of coffee-stained muslin.

1. Prepare very strong instant coffee in a bowl; soak the white muslin strips for a few seconds. (If the stain is too dark, quickly rinse the strips with clear water.) Hang them to dry.

2. Sprinkle a few drops of coffee and water on the dry strips for a nice antique effect; press.

3. Stamp 3 strips with the compass or other motif stamp, about 1½″ from one end of the strip.

4. Using the alphabet stamps, stamp 2 strips with the word *Coquillages* (or "Seashells," if you prefer English) and 2 strips with the words *à la plage* (or "at the beach"). Press to set the ink.

ASSEMBLY

1. To attach the seashells, thread some raffia through a large needle. Pull it through the linen at the top of the seashell shapes behind the white fabric rim right above the seam.

2. Tie the seashells to the twine 6″ apart. Cut the raffia ends 1½″ from the knots and fan out the strands.

3. Arrange coffee-stained strips on the twine between the seashells, fold the ends ⅞″ over the twine, and glue. Cut the ends of the strips into points as shown.

Fabric-Wrapped Wreath

This ring of prints in the colors of sea and sky, embellished with sparkly beaded beach treasures, couldn't be easier to make. Create one to hang on a door or wall, on a sheltered porch, or indoors for a welcoming touch of seaside decor.

FINISHED SIZE: 12″ diameter

ARTIST: Jeni Baker

WEBSITES: incolororder.blogspot.com
ironsea.etsy.com
flickr.com/photos/jenib

Jeni Baker loves to be creative every day, whether through photography, sewing, or quilting. She has been sewing since her mom taught her how at age 11. She sewed on and off through high school but really fell in love with crafting in college. She loves nothing more than to be surrounded by fabric! Currently she's finishing a degree in marketing and studio art. In addition to sewing, she loves to collect vintage kitchenware and bedsheets, and she sells vintage bedsheet fabric in her Etsy shop. Sewing with vintage sheets has given her a new outlook on sewing and recycling!

Materials and Supplies

- 3 turquoise print fabrics: ⅛ yard of each
- 3 lime green print fabrics: ⅛ yard of each
- 3 blue print fabrics: ⅛ yard of each
- Linen: ¼ yard
- 6 straight pins
- Variety of glass seed beads
- Beading needle
- Coordinating beading thread, such as Nymo
- Turning tool, such as a chopstick
- Fiberfill stuffing
- 12″-diameter wreath form

Cutting

TURQUOISE, LIME GREEN, AND BLUE PRINT FABRICS

Cut 1 strip 2″ × width of fabric from each print.

LINEN

Cut 1 strip 1″ × 8″ for a hanging loop.

Instructions

Note: All seam allowances are ¼".

WRAP THE WREATH

1. Remove the selvages from the print strips. Sew the strips end to end to create a long strip. Press the seams open.

2. Fold and press the strip in half lengthwise.

3. Pin one end of the fabric strip, with the folded edge facing left, to the inside curve of the wreath form.

4. Wrap the strip around the form once, covering the end of the strip. Continue wrapping, moving to the right and overlapping each wrap by approximately ½" to conceal the raw edge.

5. When you've covered the entire form, secure the end of the fabric strip with a pin.

MAKE THE EMBELLISHMENTS

1. Trace the patterns (page 113), which already include a ¼" seam allowance, and cut out templates for the shapes. Cut 2 of each shape from the linen.

2. Add beads to the top piece of each shape. Thread 12" of coordinating thread onto a beading needle and knot one end. Bring the needle up from the back at the end of one of the dashed lines shown on the patterns.

3. Add 4 seed beads to the needle and stitch back into the fabric ¼" from the first stitch. Come back up as close as possible to the previous stitch.

4. Continue to stitch, adding beads 4 at a time and following the patterns. Secure at the end with another knot. Bead all 3 shapes.

5. For each shape, place the embellished top on the bottom piece, right sides together. Pin and stitch with a ¼" seam allowance, leaving a 2" opening for turning. Backstitch at the beginning and end to secure.

6. Clip the seam allowance around the curves, and turn carefully, using a chopstick or turning tool.

7. Stuff each piece and hand sew the opening closed.

ASSEMBLE THE WREATH

1. Fold the 1″ × 8″ linen strip wrong sides together in half lengthwise; press. Using straight pins, pin the ends of the strip 4″ apart on the back of the wreath.

2. Hand stitch each embellishment in place on the front of the wreath.

Sea Turtle Quilt

FINISHED BLOCK SIZE: 5″ × 5″
FINISHED QUILT SIZE: 50″ × 60″

Mama Turtle swims with her little ones across a bold, graphic design of sea and sand. It's the perfect lap quilt for a moment of quiet relaxation, whether you're at the beach—or just wish you were!

ARTIST: Jessica Colvin

WEBSITES: insanely-crafty.blogspot.com
jmccreations.etsy.com

Jessica Colvin explores design through different media as they capture her imagination. She spent most of her childhood as a military dependent in Europe—an experience that added to her already inventive personality. She started her shop, JMC Creations, in 2008, when friends began ordering items she made as gifts. Over the years, her shop has evolved to feature mainly one-of-a-kind creations. Visit her blog, where she shares tutorials, crafting, forays into graphic design, and family adventures.

Materials and Supplies

- Linen: 1⅓ yards at 54″ width for half-square triangle (HST) blocks
- Blue shirting fabric: A variety to total 2¾ yards for HST blocks and squares
- Medium green cotton: ½ yard for appliqué
- Light green cotton: ¼ yard for appliqué
- Baby wale corduroy: 2 yards for backing
- Dark brown cotton: ⅝ yard for binding
- Batting: 58″ × 68″
- Embroidery floss (DMC 3819, 704, 3345, 905, and black)
- Perle cotton, size 5: 3 skeins each of 2 coordinating colors (DMC 312 and 3325) for quilting
- Erasable fabric marker
- Embroidery needle
- Lightweight fusible web, such as Steam-A-Seam Lite, 12″ or 16″ wide: ⅞ yard

Cutting

LINEN FABRIC

Cut 60 squares 6″ × 6″ for the HST blocks.

SHIRTING FABRICS

Cut 60 squares 6″ × 6″ for the HST blocks.

Cut 39 squares 5½″ × 5½″ for the quilt back piecing.

BACKING FABRIC

Cut a 3½″ strip from the lengthwise edge of the fabric. Reserve both pieces.

BINDING FABRIC

Cut 7 strips 2½″ × width of fabric for double-fold binding.

Instructions

Note: All seam allowances are ¼".

QUILT TOP

1. To make the half-square triangle (HST) blocks, pair a shirting and a linen 6″ × 6″ square right sides together. Draw a diagonal line across the square, and stitch ¼″ away from each side of the line.

2. Cut the triangles apart on the drawn line, press seams toward the darker fabric, and square up the HST blocks to 5½″ × 5½″. Repeat for all the 6″ × 6″ squares.

3. Arrange the HST blocks in a diamond pattern as shown in the photo.

4. Sew the HST blocks together by rows, being careful to keep them in the proper order.

QUILT BACK

1. Sew the 5½″ × 5½″ shirting squares into 3 strips of 13 squares each.

2. Sew together the shirting square strips and corduroy strips, referring to the photo for placement. The quilt back will be larger than the quilt front.

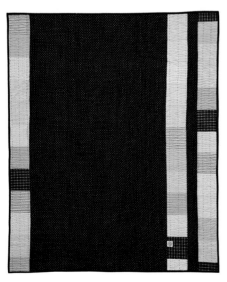

APPLIQUÉS

For stitch information, see Embroidery Stitches (page 127).

1. Trace the patterns (pages 114–116) and cut out the templates. Adding a ¼″ seam allowance, cut one each of A6, B6, and C6 from the medium green fabric and one each of A1–A5, B1–B5, and C1–C5 from the light green fabric. Cut one of each piece from the lightweight fusible web, but do not add seam allowances to these.

2. Follow the manufacturer's instructions to iron the fusible web pieces to their corresponding fabric pieces.

3. Snip the seam allowance up to the edge of the fusible web, fold over the edges to the wrong side, and press.

4. Arrange the turtles on the quilt, remove the backing from the fusible web, and iron into place.

5. Use an erasable fabric marker to mark the embroidery designs on the appliqués.

6. Embroider the edges and the designs using a running stitch; use a satin stitch for the eyes and nostrils.

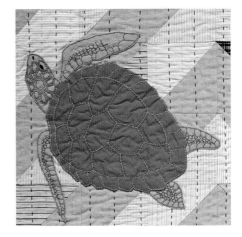

FINISHING

1. Layer and baste the quilt using your preferred method.

2. With the perle cotton, quilt by hand using rows of running stitches along the length of the quilt roughly an inch apart. Alternate the floss color from one row to the next as shown in the photos.

3. Bind the quilt using your preferred method.

Octopus and Starfish Embroidered Wall Art

A lively octopus and a twirly starfish dance and dream on dotty seas in these delightful embroideries, which are framed in wooden embroidery hoops. Tuck them among your beach finds or hang them here, there, anywhere.

FINISHED SIZE:
OCTOPUS: 5½" wide
STARFISH: 4" wide

ARTIST: Jasonda Desmond

WEBSITES: jasonda.com
dottylogic.com

Dotty Logic is the home of Jasonda Desmond's fabric collections and illustrations. Her hand-drawn designs feature vibrant lines and vivid, optimistic colors. She's inspired by nature, folk art, silly cartoon animals, and the sweet moments in everyday life. She hopes that her fabrics inspire you to craft your own beautiful and unique handmade creations.

Materials and Supplies

Yardage amounts will make both the octopus and the starfish.

- Medium-weight cotton print: fat quarter for the background
- Fabric scraps or felt for the backing
- Lightweight fusible interfacing, 20″ wide: ¼ yard
- Wood embroidery hoops: 5½″ diameter for the octopus; 4″ diameter for the starfish
- Embroidery floss: Medium pink, dark pink, and cream for the octopus; dark gold and dark gray for the starfish
- Pinking shears
- Erasable fabric marker

Cutting

MEDIUM-WEIGHT COTTON PRINT

Cut a circle 2 times the diameter of the hoop, using pinking shears.

LIGHTWEIGHT FUSIBLE INTERFACING

Cut a circle the same size as the hoop.

Instructions

Embroidery patterns are on page 25. For stitch information, see Embroidery Stitches (page 127).

1. Plan where your embroidery will fall on the fabric. For added drama, let one of the octopus legs extend beyond the hoop or place your starfish off-center. Center the fusible interfacing circle on the wrong side of the fabric circle under where you want the embroidery to be. Press according to the manufacturer's directions.

2. Use an erasable fabric marker to mark the embroidery pattern on the right side of the fabric, over the area that is backed with interfacing.

3. Place the fabric circle in the hoop and tighten. Embroider the pattern on the fabric. For the octopus, use a backstitch for the outlines and French knots on the arms and in the eyes. For the starfish, use a chain stitch in the center of each arm, seed stitch to fill, and whipstitch for the outline. Restretch the fabric and tighten the hoop as the fabric becomes loose.

4. To finish the back, use embroidery floss to sew a loose (approximately ⅛″ long) running stitch around the fabric circle, about ¼″ from the edge. Gather the fabric as you sew. Pull tight to draw the fabric toward the center and knot securely.

5. Cut a small circle of scrap fabric or felt to cover the back and the gathered edge. Tack it in place using cotton thread.

6. To make a hanger for the wall display, sew a loop with embroidery floss about 1″ from the top on the back; knot securely. Alternatively, attach a safety pin to the back to create a quick hanger.

Starfish and octopus
embroidery patterns

This area extends beyond hoop.

Whale of a Pillow

In this pillow tale, Moby Dick is a friendly whale, ready to swim in perfect harmony across a chair or bed. He makes a cute soft toy, too!

FINISHED SIZE: Approximately 10″ long × 6″ high at tail

ARTIST: Kate Durkin

WEBSITES: katedurkin.com
katedurkin.etsy.com

Kate Durkin is a New York–based textile artist and painter. She opened her business, katedurkin, in 2007, offering hand-crafted embroidered pillows featuring owls, giraffes, whales, bunnies, foxes, and other creatures, as well as original paintings and prints. Kate sells her products through her Etsy shop, in stores across the country, and at local markets.

Materials and Supplies

- Ivory cotton canvas: 1 piece 11″ × 14″
- Cotton print fabric: 1 piece 11″ × 14″
- Embroidery floss in dark brown and red
- Small (5″–6″) embroidery hoop and needle
- Erasable fabric marking pencil
- Fiberfill stuffing

Instructions

For stitch information, see Embroidery Stitches (page 127).

1. Trace the pattern (page 29) and cut out a template. With an erasable fabric marking pencil, draw around the template onto the ivory cotton canvas, allowing at least 3″ of fabric around the outline. Mark the embroidery design on the fabric.

2. Place the fabric in the embroidery hoop. Referring to the photo for the colors, start at any point and use a running stitch to sew the whale and star outlines and the lines of the eye. Each stitch should be about ¼″. Then reverse the stitching direction and follow the line back to the beginning, filling in the blank spaces until you have a solid line. Use a satin stitch to complete the eye.

3. Remove from the hoop. Press. On the back, draw a line around the image, about 1½″ outside the outline.

4. Place the cotton print fabric right side up and place the embroidered piece wrong side up on top. Pin and machine stitch them together along the drawn outline, leaving a small opening at the bottom for turning. Trim the seam allowance to about ¼″. Clip the seam allowances at the curves.

5. Turn the piece right side out, press, and stuff. Sew the opening closed.

6. Cut a 2″ × 3″ rectangle from the ivory cotton canvas; turn under and press its edges. Hand stitch it over the opening to create a clean, finished look.

Whale embroidery pattern. Enlarge 200%.

Sailboat Stuffie

FINISHED SIZE: 8½″ high × 6″ across at base

A deep-sea-blue sailboat finds a berth as a stylish doorstop.
Or stuff it with fiberfill instead of rice or sand, and it can be
a fun companion for the Whale of a Pillow (page 26).

ARTIST: Kate Durkin

WEBSITES: katedurkin.com
katedurkin.etsy.com

For more about Kate, see
her artist bio (page 27).

Materials and Supplies

- Blue cotton canvas:
  1 piece 12″ × 14″
- Cotton print fabric:
  1 piece 11″ × 14″
- Embroidery floss in white,
  tan, blue, and red
- White thread
- Small (5″–6″) embroi-
  dery hoop and needle
- Erasable fabric
  marking pencil
- Rice or sand (or fiberfill
  stuffing for a pillow)

Instructions

For stitch information, see Embroidery Stitches (page 127).

1. Trace the pattern (page 116) and cut out a template. With an erasable fabric pencil, draw around the template on the blue cotton canvas, allowing at least 3″ of fabric around the outline. Mark the embroidery design on the fabric.

2. Place the fabric in the embroi-dery hoop. Refer to the photos (page 30 and right) for floss colors. Starting at any point, use a running stitch to stitch along the sailboat and star outlines. Each stitch should be about ¼″. Then, reverse the stitching direction and follow the line back to the beginning, filling in the blank spaces until you have a completed line. Stitch the slats at the bottom of the boat using the same technique and white thread.

3. Remove from the hoop. Press. On the back, draw a line around the image, about 1½″ outside the outline.

4. Place the cotton print fabric right side up and the embroi-dered piece *wrong* side up on top. Pin and machine stitch them together along the drawn outline, leaving a small opening at the bottom for turning. Trim the seam allow-ance to about ¼″. Clip the seam allowance at the curves.

5. Turn the piece right side out, press, and stuff. Sew the opening closed.

6. Cut a 2″ × 3″ rectangle from the blue cotton canvas, turn under and press its edges. Hand stitch it over the opening to create a clean, finished look.

Deep Waters Quilt

FINISHED QUILT SIZE: *40″ × 48″*

Off on the horizon, a little boat skims across the deep blue-green sea, while a sea bird sails the skies above. Use simple paper piecing to put them together on this quilt—a bright and cheery gift for a child or anyone in your life.

ARTIST: Chrissy Foy

WEBSITES: hicketypicketyhandmade.com
hicketypicketyHM.etsy.com

Chrissy Foy is a crafter, blogger, and mom who calls the "Nature Coast" of Florida home. While she has always enjoyed creating, it wasn't until she had children of her own that she fell head-over-heels in love with sewing. Chrissy loves the challenge and satisfaction that comes with creating her own patterns, and she is passionate about exploring new techniques and perfecting her workmanship. The natural beauty of her surroundings and her two young daughters provide endless inspiration. Most of her work can be found on her blog and is sometimes available for purchase at her Etsy shop.

Materials and Supplies

- White fabric: ½ yard for top strip
- Coordinating solid or printed scraps for the boat and sail
- Coordinating solid or printed scraps for the bird
- Five different sea-green and blue fabrics for the ocean: ¼ yard each
- Tan or beige fabric for the sand: ¼ yard
- Backing fabric: 1⅝ yards*
- Binding fabric: ½ yard
- Batting: 44″ × 52″
- Thin paper: 2 sheets 8½″ × 11″ for piecing the boat and bird (Regular printer paper works fine.)
  Requires 44″ fabric width

Cutting

Cut 2 pieces 7½″ × 10½″ (sections 1 and 3).

Cut 1 piece 10½″ × 4¾″ (section 2).

Cut 1 piece 5¼″ × 1¾″ (section 4).

Cut 1 piece 5¼″ × 7″ (section 5).

Cut 1 piece 11¼″ × 10½″ (section 6).

Cut 2 pieces 4″ × 4½″ (boat blocks A2 and A3).

Cut 1 strip 2″ × 10¾″ (boat block A4).

Cut 2 pieces 3″ × 4″ (boat blocks B2 and B3).

Cut 2 pieces 4″ × 5″ (boat blocks B4 and B5).

Cut 1 piece 3″ × 2″ (bird block C2).

Cut 1 piece 4½″ × 3½″ (bird block C4).

Cut 1 piece 4″ × 3½″ (bird block C5).

Cut 1 strip 4½″ × 1½″ (bird block D1).

Cut 1 square 2″ × 2″ (bird block D3).

BOAT FABRICS

Cut 1 strip 4″ × 10″ (boat block A1).

Cut 1 square 4″ × 4″ (boat block B1).

BIRD FABRICS

Cut 1 piece 3″ × 2″ (bird block C1).

Cut 1 piece 2½″ × 3″ (bird block C3).

Cut 1 square 2½″ × 2½″ (bird block D2).

GREEN AND BLUE FABRICS

Cut 1 strip 8½″ × 40″ (section 7).

Cut 1 strip 6¾″ × 40″ (section 8).

Cut 1 strip 4¾″ × 40″ (section 9).

Cut 1 strip 5¾″ × 40″ (section 10).

Cut 1 strip 8¼″ × 40″ (section 11).

TAN FABRIC

Cut 1 strip 6½″ × 40″ (section 12).

BINDING FABRIC

Cut 5 strips 2½″ × width of fabric for double-fold binding.

Quilt diagram

Instructions

All seam allowances are ¼" and are included unless stated otherwise.

QUILT TOP ASSEMBLY

1. Copy the boat pattern (page 117) onto paper and cut it out. Cut along the dotted line to create 2 pieces.

2. Use your favorite paper-piecing method to assemble each part of the boat pattern. Leave ¼" of fabric beyond the dotted line on each section for seam allowances.

3. Using the paper as a guide, trim any excess fabric, except along the dotted line. Leave a ¼" seam allowance along the dotted line. Tear the paper away from the fabric.

4. Place the 2 block pieces right sides together, aligning the raw edges along the dotted line. Sew and press the seam to one side.

5. Repeat Steps 1–4 for the bird block (pattern on page 117).

6. Refer to the quilt diagram (page 34) and sew the boat block to quilt section 2.

7. Sew the bird block to quilt sections 4 and 5.

8. Sew sections 1, 3, and 6 to the boat and bird blocks.

9. Add the ocean sections, one at a time, and add the sand strip.

10. Trim the quilt top so sides are straight and corners are square.

QUILTING AND FINISHING

1. Mark quilting designs as desired on the quilt top or plan to quilt without marking.

2. Layer and baste the quilt using your preferred method.

3. Quilt by hand or machine.

4. Bind the quilt using your preferred method.

Seashore Sunhat

FINISHED SIZE: about 18″ in diameter

*Stitch up a little shade for a sunny day at the beach with this soft
and simple hat, shown here made in fresh hues of sky blue and leafy
green. Line it in a coordinating fabric for a fun touch.*

ARTIST: Jona Giammalva

WEBSITES: fabritopia.com
jonag.typepad.com

Jona Giammalva shares her fabric and sewing adventures on her blog "Stop Staring and Start Sewing!" and owns a little store called Fabritopia. An avid sewer for more than 25 years, she recently began producing sewing patterns of her original designs under the name Jona G. Pattern Co. When not chasing her five kids or spray painting everything in sight, she can be found at her Arizona home dabbling in her newly acquired quilting hobby.

Materials and Supplies

- ⅔ yard of fabric for hat exterior
- ⅔ yard of fabric for hat lining
- ⅛ yard of fabric for side accent strips
- ⅛ yard of fabric for neck strap
- 2½ yards of 20″-wide lightweight interfacing
- ⅔ yard of 45″-wide heavyweight interfacing, such as Pellon 809 Decor Bond, for the brim
- 2 cord stops or beads (Jona used seashells with holes that are big enough to pull the strap through.)

Cutting

NECK STRAP FABRIC

Cut 1 strip 1″ × width of fabric.

Instructions

Template patterns are on page 118. All seam allowances are ¼".

1. Enlarge the crown section pattern and the side accent strips pattern. Create templates.

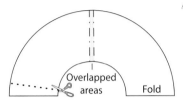

Enlarge and print 2 of the brim patterns; cut out and tape them together so that the shaded areas overlap. Cut along the line on one edge (the other edge will be placed on the fold). Create a template from this pattern.

2. Fold over the exterior hat fabric at least 10". Place the brim template on the fold and cut. Repeat with the lining fabric and the heavyweight interfacing. Cut 2 from the heavyweight interfacing.

3. Follow the manufacturer's instructions to apply the lightweight interfacing to the remaining exterior and lining fabric and to the side accent strip fabric. Cut out the remaining pattern pieces: 6 crown sections from interfaced exterior fabric, 6 crown sections from interfaced lining fabric, and 4 interfaced side accent strips on a fold.

4. To sew the exterior crown, place 2 pieces right sides together and stitch on one side. Press the seams open and stitch on a third piece. Repeat with the other 3 pieces. Sew the 2 sections together.

5. Repeat Step 4 with the lining fabric crown pieces.

6. Fold over the short ends of all 4 side accent strips by ¼"; press, and stitch.

7. Pin 2 side accent strips to the exterior crown with right sides together, leaving a ¼" gap on each side.

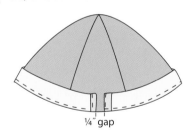

Sew in place. Repeat with the remaining 2 accent strips and the lining crown.

8. Follow the manufacturer's directions to apply heavyweight interfacing to each brim piece. Place the ends right sides together and stitch to close the "circle."

9. Pin the inside of the exterior brim to the exterior side accent strips with right sides together, aligning

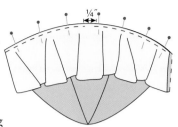

the seam at the back of the crown with the brim seam. Use lots of pins to get it placed just right. Stitch all the way around. Be sure to leave a ¼″ gap in the stitching on each side where the brim meets the side strips. Repeat for the lining brim.

10. On the back of each brim, ¼″ from the outer edge, stitch a line 4″ long. Place the hat and its lining right sides together. Pin well along the outer edges of the brim.

11. Sew the 2 sides together along the outer edge of the brim, leaving an opening along the 4″ stitched line from Step 10. Snip tiny notches along the brim every 3″. Turn the hat right side out.

12. Fold under along the 4″ stitched line and press well.

13. Slipstitch around both ¼″ gaps.

14. Stitch close to the edge of the brim all the way around, stitching the 4″ hole closed. Stitch ½″ from the previous stitch line; repeat all the way to the top of the brim.

15. Pin together the exterior and lining side accent strips. Stitch at the top and bottom of each accent strip close to each seam.

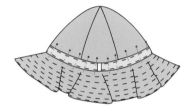

16. Fold the neck strap fabric strip in half lengthwise, wrong sides together, and press. Open it back up and fold in each side ¼″; press. Fold it back in half and press again. Stitch along the edge with the double folds.

17. Tie a knot at the center of the neck strap. Pull the ends through one of the beads or shells, and cinch all the way to the knot.

18. Place the knot and the bead or shell on top of the brim at the back of the hat. Pull the ends through the gaps at the hat sides; then pull on the other bead or shell. Tie a knot under the bead or shell, and trim the ends.

Rainbow Fish

FINISHED SIZE: Approximately 3½″ × 11″

Rub-a-dub-dub, two fish in a tub…These vibrant felt fish are perfectly at home out of water. Set them on your mantel or windowsill. Or plop them in a bucket. Add them anywhere you want a "splash" of bright color to liven up your decor.

ARTIST: Abby Glassenberg

WEBSITES: abbyglassenberg.com
whileshenaps.typepad.com

Abby Glassenberg is a textile artist, mother, and teacher who creates one-of-a-kind soft toys and sculptures in her home studio in Massachusetts. Sixteen of her soft sculpture birds are featured in Abby's book, *The Artful Bird: Feathered Friends to Make and Sew*, available at booksellers nationwide. Abby still sews on a sewing machine that she bought when she was thirteen years old. Nature is a continual source of inspiration for Abby, as are her three little girls, Roxanne, Stella, and Josephine. To learn more about Abby's sewing and her life, visit her blog; to see her portfolio, please visit her website.

Materials and Supplies

- Scraps of wool felt in cream and various rainbow colors
- Brown embroidery floss: about 12″
- Fiberfill stuffing
- Turning tool, such as a chopstick
- Disappearing fabric marker or tailor's chalk
- Fabric glue
- Embroidery needle

Instructions

1. Trace the patterns (page 119), including all markings, and cut out templates for all the pieces. Cut 2 heads from cream felt and 2 bodies from any color, adding a ¼″ seam allowance to each piece. Cut 1 outer tail piece, 2 middle tail pieces, 2 inner tail pieces, 1 top fin piece, 2 middle fin pieces, and 2 lower fin pieces from various colors. Do not add a seam allowance to these pieces. Cut slits in the body and top fin pieces as indicated on the patterns. Cut 2 eyes from cream felt and 2 eyeballs from green felt.

2. Use a disappearing fabric marker or tailor's chalk to transfer the markings on the body for lower fin and top fin placement.

3. Place the top fin upside down on a body piece so that the top body edge and bottom fin edge are aligned. Ease around the curve. Baste.

4. Place the lower fins on top of one another, upside down on top of the body piece. Align the bottom body edge with the upper fin edge; baste.

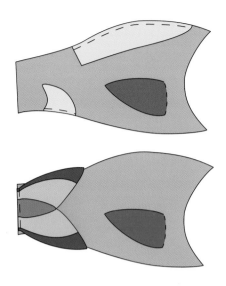

5. Insert a middle fin through the slit in the fish body. Fold over the body and stitch across the slit, catching the fin in the seam. Repeat for the other fish body.

6. Sandwich the outer tail between the 2 middle and 2 inner tails; baste.

7. Place the tail "sandwich" upside down on top of the body piece that does not have the upper and lower fins basted to it; baste.

8. Place a fish head against the right side of a fish body and pin from point A to point B, easing around the curve. Stitch. Repeat for the other head and body.

9. Pin the 2 fish head/body pieces right sides together. Stitch around edges from point C to point D, catching the top and lower fins and the tail in the seam. Trim the seam allowance to ⅛″ and carefully clip the curves close to the stitching.

10. Turn the body right side out through the opening. Use a chopstick or turning tool to gently push each fin completely right side out.

11. Stuff the fish firmly, using small wads of stuffing. Close the opening with tiny ladder stitches (see Embroidery Stitches on page 127); remove all basting stitches.

12. Glue the eyeballs to the eyes with fabric glue; then glue the eyes to the fish.

13. With brown embroidery floss, embroider a mouth with one long stitch, tying small knots at the base of the smile on both sides.

Sparkly Starfish

FINISHED SIZE: Approximately 6½″ wide

Real starfish occur in a rainbow of colors, including ochre, orange, white, red, and even deep blue. So feel free to make yours in any colors you wish. Then embellish with seed beads that will sparkle like drops of water from the sea.

ARTIST: Abby Glassenberg

WEBSITES: abbyglassenberg.com
        whileshenaps.typepad.com

For more about Abby, see
her artist bio (page 41).

Materials and Supplies

- Wool felt in 2 colors: at least $6\frac{1}{2}''$ × $6\frac{1}{2}''$ each
- Seed beads in a color that coordinates with the felt: about 60
- Fiberfill stuffing
- Turning tool, such as a chopstick
- Beading needle
- Coordinating beading thread, such as Nymo

Instructions

1. Trace the pattern (page 120), and cut out the template. Cut 1 starfish body piece from each felt square.

2. Pin, and then stitch together the body pieces from point A to point B. Trim the seam allowance to ⅛", and carefully clip curves very close to the stitching.

3. Turn the body right side out through the opening by first pulling each starfish arm into the body cavity and then gently pulling the arms out through the opening. Use a chopstick or turning tool to gently push each arm completely right side out.

4. Begin with the arms and stuff firmly; close the opening with tiny ladder stitches (see Embroidery Stitches on page 127).

5. To attach the seed beads, insert a threaded hand-sewing needle through the top middle of the starfish's body, coming up close to the center. Tug on the thread to pull the knot into the body.

6. Thread a seed bead onto the needle and pull it down flush with the starfish's body. Insert the needle into the starfish, directly next to seed bead, coming up ⅛″ away along one of the starfish's arms. Thread a second seed bead and continue in this manner, using the dots indicated on the pattern as a guide, until all 5 arms are embellished with seed beads.

Cuddle Me Seahorse

With its dragonlike scales, horselike head, and wing-like fin, even a real seahorse looks like a mythical creature. To make the most of its fanciful charm, use bright colors and print fabric to create this curly-tailed seahorse stuffie—the perfect cuddly bedtime friend for any child.

FINISHED SIZE: Approximately 15″ high

ARTIST: Nathalia Gunawan

WEBSITES: liaspace.com
sewmanics.com

By day, Nathalia (Lia) Gunawan is a furniture manufacturer and interior contractor, as well as a full-time mother of two. At night, when the children are asleep, she's a crafter and seamstress. Lia and her business partner, Chia, own Sewmanics, a children's clothing business. Sewmanics was created through the two friends' passion for sewing and fabrics, as well as their love for their children.

Materials and Supplies

- Red print: 2 pieces 11½″ × 16½″ for seahorse body
- Green corduroy: 2 pieces 5″ × 5½″ for fin
- Batting or stabilizer: 5″ × 5½″ for fin
- Scraps of white and black felt for eyes
- Fiberfill stuffing

Instructions

Note: All seam allowances are ⅜".

1. Trace the patterns (page 121), join the 2 body patterns, and cut out templates for the pieces. With right sides of the fabric together, cut out 2 body pieces from the red print, 2 fin pieces from the green corduroy, and 1 fin piece from the batting. Cut 2 large eye circles from white felt and 2 small eye circles from black felt.

2. Place the fin corduroy pieces right sides together. Place the fin batting piece on the wrong side of a corduroy piece. Stitch around the edges, leaving the straight side open. Trim the seam allowances and clip the curves.

3. Turn the fin right side out and topstitch around the edges. Refer to the photo (page 48) for decorative free-motion stitching ideas.

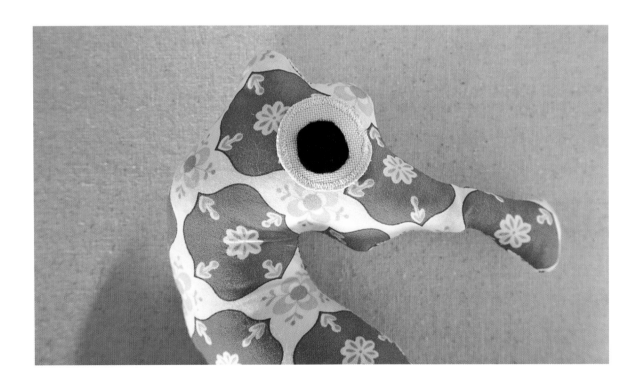

4. Machine stitch a white and a black eye to each body piece, following the diamond pattern shown on the eye on the seahorse pattern (page 121).

5. Place the body pieces right sides together, with the fin sandwiched inside and with the fin's straight edge aligned with the body edges. Stitch all around the body, leaving a gap where indicated on the pattern. Clip the curves and turn right side out. For easier turning, before stitching sandwich embroidery floss (approx. 10″) at the edge of the tail, making sure it follows the curl of the tail and does not get sewn over except at the very end of the tail. Make a knot at the outside end of the floss. When you turn the body, slowly pull the embroidery floss to make an easy and perfect tail turn.

6. Stuff the polyester filling into the body; use a chopstick or other similar tool to push little bits of fiberfill into the tail. Hand stitch to close the gap.

Courteous Crab Napkin Wraps

FINISHED SIZE: 3¾" × 2¾"

Create that authentic crab shack atmosphere with a casual table setting featuring these jaunty napkin ties. Wrapped around bright red napkins, the friendly embroidered crab and rope ties add seaside flair.

ARTIST: Mollie Johanson

WEBSITES: wildolive.blogspot.com
wildolive.etsy.com
flickr.com/photos/molliejohanson/

Mollie Johanson, a trained graphic designer specializing in print projects, began her blog Wild Olive as an outlet for more whimsical works. Daily dreaming and doodling have resulted in a variety of embroidery and paper projects, most featuring simply expressive faces. Mollie, based in a far western suburb of Chicago, commutes daily to her in-home studio via the coffeepot.

Materials and Supplies

Makes 1 napkin wrap.

- Lightweight canvas or heavy cotton: 3″ × 4″
- Wool felt: 3″ × 4″
- Red, orange, and black embroidery floss
- Embroidery needle
- Rope-style trim: 12″
- Liquid seam sealant, such as Dritz Fray Check (optional)

Instructions

Embroidery pattern is below.

1. Trace the crab pattern onto the canvas. Use 3 strands of floss and the backstitch to embroider all the lines. Use French knots for the eyes and 1 backstitch for each spot. Do not sew the orange running stitch around the edges yet. For stitch information, see Embroidery Stitches (page 127).

2. Layer together the embroidered canvas and the felt. Trim both layers into an oval, leaving a border of approximately ¼″ around the crab. If you wish, you can seal the edges of the canvas with a liquid seam sealant. Set aside the canvas piece.

3. Knot both ends of the rope trim tightly. Find the center of the rope trim and hand sew the center to the middle of the back of the felt.

4. Line up the canvas over the felt, and hand sew the canvas and felt together around the outside with orange floss, using a running stitch.

Crab embroidery pattern

Jolly Buccaneer Shirt

Ahoy, mateys! This appliquéd ship in full sail lends seaworthy spirit aplenty to a T-shirt for your little pirate.

FINISHED SIZE: 7¼″ × 6¾″

ARTIST: Heather Jones

WEBSITES: oliveandollie.com
oliveandollie.etsy.com

Heather Jones is a designer, seamstress, and quilter. Her business, Olive & Ollie, specializes in modern, wearable clothing and accessories for infants and children. Heather sells her handmade designs in her Etsy shop and at select U.S. retail locations. She also is working on her first line of appliqué, sewing, and quilting patterns. She is founder and current president of the Cincinnati Modern Quilt Guild, and her original quilt *Yield* won the guild's Project Modern Challenge 1. Heather's husband, Jeff, and children, Aidan and Olivia, are her biggest supporters and greatest sources of inspiration.

Materials and Supplies

- T-shirt
- Blue dot fabric: 8″ × 8″ for body of ship, masts, and crosstree
- White solid fabric: 3″ × 8″ for sails
- Red tonal fabric: 3″ × 3″ for flags
- Lightweight fusible web, such as HeatnBond Lite, 12″ or 16″ wide: ⅓ yard
- Tear-away stabilizer (optional)
- Threads to match fabrics

Instructions

1. Iron fusible web to the wrong side of each piece of fabric, following the manufacturer's instructions.

2. Trace the patterns (page 57) and cut out templates. Place them wrong side up on the back of the prepared fabrics, trace the outlines on the paper backing, and cut out.

3. Remove the paper and lay out the design on the T-shirt front. Adjust the lengths of the outer 2 masts as needed by trimming the ends so they lie just beneath the ship piece. Layer the sails, flags, and crosstree over the masts.

4. Fuse the pieces to the T-shirt, following the manufacturer's instructions.

5. Optional: Turn the T-shirt wrong side out and iron on tear-away stabilizer behind the entire design, following the manufacturer's instructions. Turn the T-shirt right side out.

6. Stitch along the edges of each appliqué piece, using a tight zigzag stitch and thread to match each fabric color. Backstitch at the end of each section to secure the threads.

7. Carefully remove the tear-away stabilizer, if used, and snip any loose threads.

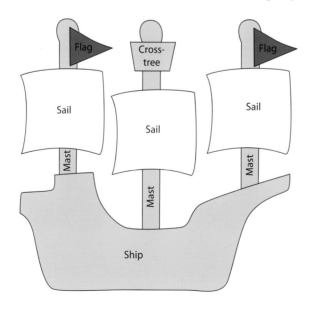

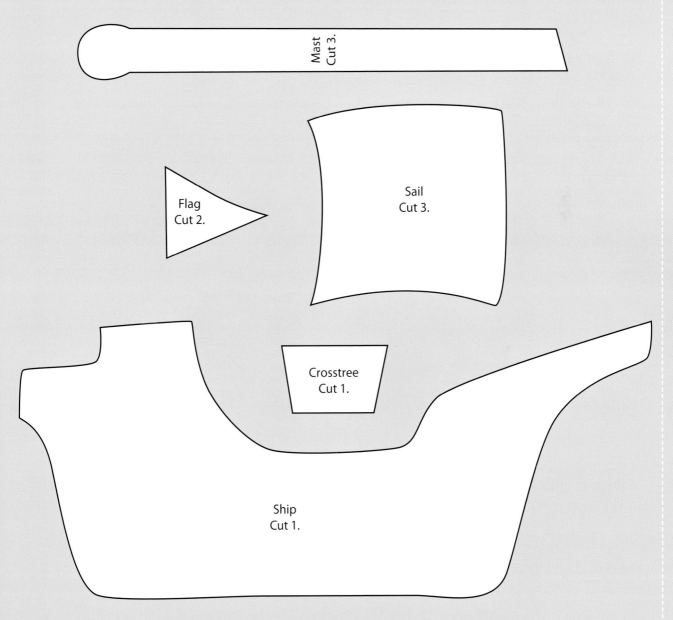

Mast
Cut 3.

Flag
Cut 2.

Sail
Cut 3.

Crosstree
Cut 1.

Ship
Cut 1.

Jolly Buccaneer patterns

Cast Your Nets Appliqué

The homespun textures and free-and-easy stitching in this charming little wall adornment are a gentle reminder of things nautical. Use your imagination and your own choice of embellishments to make it your own.

FINISHED SIZE: 10" × 10"

ARTIST: Priscilla Jones

WEBSITES: priscillajones.wordpress.com
priscillajones.blogspot.com/
facebook.com/#!/priscilla.jones2
twitter.com/#!/priscillajones
flickr.com/photos/38187919@N08/

Priscilla Jones has been producing contemporary embroidered textiles since completing her degree in embroidery at Manchester Metropolitan University in 1997. Her work focuses on the use of found materials to evoke personal memories of her childhood and love of sewing. Inspired by the faded beauty of her surroundings on England's north-west coast, she works with soft tones and textures, as well as nostalgic imagery from a bygone era. Priscilla's work has been featured in several books, and her pieces are sold and exhibited across the world, with many held in public and private collections. Priscilla has developed her quirky embroidered designs into a range of greeting cards, wallpaper, and fashion and decorating fabrics. She also lectures on embroidery and textiles and runs independent workshops demonstrating her techniques and processes.

Materials and Supplies

Use lightweight cotton or linen for this project.

- Pale green solid fabric: 10″ × 10″ for the background
- White, lilac, beige, and pale blue solid fabrics: a total of 6½″ × 6½″ for the middle background
- Red dotted fabric: 3″ × 4″ for the boat
- Brown dotted fabric: 2″ × 2½″ for the boat
- Blue striped fabric: 3″ × 3″ for the cabin
- Red solid fabric: 2″ × 4″ for the life ring and flag
- Light blue striped fabric: 2″ × 3″ for the bunting
- White solid fabric: 2″ × 3″ for the cabin window and life ring
- Cotton sewing machine threads in light blue, turquoise, red, and cerise pink*
- Light blue hand embroidery thread
- Lightweight fusible web (17″ wide): ½ yard
- Tear-away fabric stabilizer: 11″ × 11″
- Water-soluble fabric marker
- Buttons or beads

*If desired, use rayon embroidery thread; it gives a nice sheen to your stitching.

Instructions

1. Trace the patterns (page 61), and cut out the templates. Layer the pale green solid fabric and stabilizer for the background, and pin together with the fabric right side up.

2. Cut out as desired or as shown below, and arrange the pale solid background fabrics, fusible web side down, on the pale green background in a square measuring approximately 6½″ × 6½″. Fuse with a hot iron according to the manufacturer's instructions.

3. Fuse the fusible web to the wrong sides of the remaining fabrics, following the manufacturer's instructions. Trace around the pattern pieces with a water-soluble marker and cut them out. Peel off the backing paper from all the pieces.

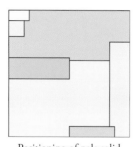

Positioning of pale solid background fabrics

4. Place the boat, cabin, bunting, and other pieces over the background fabrics and fuse. (If your fabrics are moving around and not fusing together, increase the temperature of your iron and apply more heat.)

5. Using light blue thread, sew along the edges of the pale solid background fabrics. Change to red thread and carefully stitch around the boat's inside edge. Change to turquoise thread and continue to sew until the boat and the bunting are complete. If you wish, you can create more intense lines by stitching over your lines more than once. Refer to the photo (page 58) for additional stitching ideas.

6. Using the cerise thread, add text. (Try it out first on a separate piece of fabric until you like the results.)

7. Run a line of straight stitching about ½″ inside the edges of the pale green background fabric. Then fray the edging by carefully pulling out the threads nearest the cut edge.

8. Refer to the photo (page 58) to add hand stitching. For stitch information, see Embroidery Stitches (page 127). Add buttons or beads as a finishing touch. Using old odd buttons gives the image a quirky, handmade vintage look.

9. Remove the stabilizer from the back and give the piece a good pressing on the reverse with a hot iron.

Cast Your Nets patterns

Saucy Mermaid

FINISHED SIZE: Approximately 5″ × 15″

From her perch on the rocks, this cheeky little mermaid issues her own whimsical version of a siren call. She's certainly got her own style, from her flowing green felt hair to those multicolored scales.

ARTIST: Heidi Kenney

WEBSITE: mypapercrane.com

Heidi Kenney is a self-taught artist who creates plush and three-dimensional soft sculptures—happy (and sometimes very sad) plush veggies, donuts, toilet paper roll dolls, and other everyday food and household items. Heidi started her company and website, My Paper Crane, in 2001. Her first book, *Every Day's A Holiday*, was released in 2010 with Chronicle Books. Her work has been featured in the *New York Times, The Boston Globe,* and *Print* magazine. She has participated in group exhibitions around the globe, including in Tokyo, Australia, and the United Kingdom. Heidi recently had her second solo show, "If You Lived Here, You Would Be Home," in Seattle, Washington. She currently collaborates with the company Kidrobot to create key chains and plush pillows.

Materials and Supplies

- Cream felt, 36″ wide: ½ yard
- Green felt in various shades, 36″ wide: to total ¼ yard
- Gold felt: 6″ × 8″
- Black felt: 1″ × 1½″
- White felt: 1½″ × 2½″
- Pink felt: 1″ × 2″
- Coral felt: 1″ × 2″
- Pink embroidery floss
- Fiberfill stuffing
- Fabric glue

Instructions

1. Trace the patterns (pages 122 and 123), and cut out templates for all the pieces.

2. Cut out the body, head pieces, nose, and eyelids from the cream felt. Use white for the eyes and eye highlights, black for the pupils, pink for the cheeks, and coral for the shell bra. Cut the scales, hair, and tail from the gold and greens.

3. Pin the long head strip around the edges of an oval head piece. Stitch together using a ¼″ seam allowance, and then pin and stitch to the other oval head piece, leaving a small opening for turning. Turn right side out. Stuff. Hand stitch the opening closed. Set aside.

4. Sew together the 2 body pieces using a ¼″ seam allowance, leaving the neck open. Clip the seam allowance at the curves. Turn and stuff.

5. Turn under the edge of the neck opening, and pin the open neck to the bottom of the head. Hand stitch firmly together.

6. Glue the tail pieces to the bottom of the body.

7. Glue the scales to the body. Begin at the waist and overlap the scales as you go, staggering the colors. Allow to dry.

8. Use embroidery floss and a backstitch to stitch a small mouth. (Draw it lightly in pencil first if you wish.) You can hide your end stitches behind the eyes and cheeks. For stitch information, see Embroidery Stitches (page 127).

9. Glue on the eyes, cheeks, nose, and shell bra. Allow to dry.

10. Arrange the hair pieces as desired and glue them in place. Cut a couple more pieces if needed to cover any bare areas.

Starfish Appliqué Handbag

Softly sophisticated, this handbag with its starfish motif will remind you of that time at the shore no matter where you happen to be.

FINISHED SIZE: Approximately 15″ × 11″ × 3″

ARTIST: Laura Obiso

WEBSITE: LauraOhDesigns.etsy.com

Laura Obiso is a New Jersey native with more than 50 years of sewing experience. She grew up with fabrics: In 1950, her parents opened a small fabric remnant store that steadily grew to become the largest fabric center in northern New Jersey. She has a love for beautiful fabrics and the creative process, and she spends most of her day in the studio. Through her business, LauraOh Designs, she also makes primitive dolls and home decor items, so her sewing machine is rarely idle.

Materials and Supplies

Quilting cottons or lightweight decorator fabrics work best for this project.

- Striped fabric: ¾ yard for the bag exterior and inner pocket
- Solid coordinating fabric: ¾ yard for the bag lining, inner pocket lining, and bag handles
- Coordinating light-colored fabric: 6″ × 12″ piece for starfish appliqué
- Cotton webbing, 1″ wide: 1⅓ yards for the 24″ bag handles (12″ drop)

- Lightweight* fusible interfacing: ¾ yard
- Lightweight* quilt batting: ¾ yard
- Magnetic snap closure
- Swivel latch for keys
- Freezer paper
- Erasable fabric pencil

This handbag is designed to be "slouchy" and soft. For a more stand-up type of bag, use a heavier weight interfacing, quilt batting, or both.

Cutting

STRIPED FABRIC

Cut 2 pieces 16″ × 12″ for the bag exterior.

Cut 1 piece 16″ × 6½″ for the pocket.

Cut 1 piece 4″ × 8″ for the snap closure tab.

SOLID COORDINATING FABRIC

Cut 2 pieces 16″ × 12″ for the lining.

Cut 1 piece 16″ × 6½″ for the pocket lining.

Cut 2 strips 2″ × 24″ for the handles.*

Cut 1 piece 4″ × 8″ for the snap closure tab.

Cut 1 piece 1½″ × 6″ for the swivel latch.

WEBBING

Cut 2 pieces, each 24″ long.

INTERFACING AND BATTING

Cut 2 pieces, each 16″ × 12″.

Or cut to your desired handle length.

Instructions

Note: All seam allowances are ½″ unless stated otherwise.

BAG EXTERIOR

1. Trace 2 of the starfish pattern (page 124) onto the freezer paper's dull side. Press them shiny side down on the wrong side of the coordinating light-colored fabric; cut out.

2. Arrange the 2 starfish on the lower left corner of the bag exterior front; allow about 3″ from the bottom and side for seams and turning. When you are pleased with the placement, remove the top starfish and set aside.

3. Remove the freezer paper from the bottom starfish and pin or press the starfish on the fabric to hold it in place. (The waxy film left behind by the freezer paper will lightly hold the appliqué in place.)

4. Machine stitch around the edges of the bottom starfish. (Laura used a decorative feather stitch.)

5. Repeat Steps 3 and 4 with the second starfish. Press both starfish.

6. Fuse interfacing to the wrong side of both bag exterior pieces, following the manufacturer's instructions. Place the quilt batting on top of the interfacing and baste around the edges, using a ¼″ seam allowance. Press.

7. Place the exterior pieces right sides together. Sew along both sides and across the bottom. Press the seam allowances open.

8. To box the bottom corners, match the side and bottom seams at the corners and pin. Sew straight across about 1½″ from the tip. Clip the corner points and press. Turn the bag right side out. Set aside.

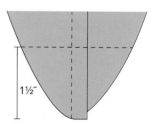

1½″

MAGNETIC SNAP TABS

1. Fold each lining piece in half (side to side) and mark the bag center at the top with chalk or a pin.

2. Fold the tab pieces in half lengthwise wrong sides together; press flat. Open, fold the long edges to the pressed center line, and press. Now fold the piece in half, short ends together, and press again.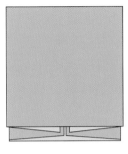

3. Place a tab on the right side of a lining piece, with center lines matching and short raw edges of the tab even with the lining's top raw edge. Pin securely. Topstitch the tab to the lining on all sides of the tab, about ¼″ from the edges.

4. Repeat Step 3 with the second tab and the other lining piece. The tabs should align with each other when the linings are placed together.

5. Measure about 2½″ down from the top edge of the lining and mark the center of the tab. Attach the magnetic closure according to the manufacturer's directions. On the wrong side of the lining, place about a 1″ × 1″ square of quilt batting over the closure prongs for

extra padding. When half of the magnet is in place, snap the halves together and lay out the lining, making sure the tab placement is correct before securing the second half of the closure to the second bag lining tab.

POCKET AND LINING

1. Use either the bag exterior fabric or the lining fabric as the outside of the pocket. Pin the pocket pieces right sides together. Sew together along both long edges. Turn and press.

2. Pin the pocket right side up to the right side of a lining piece about halfway down the bag, just under the snap tab. Match the short ends of the pocket with the lining piece's side edges.

3. Sew the pocket to the lining along the side edges, using a ¼″ seam allowance. Decide where you would like sections to be on the pockets and mark lightly with an erasable fabric pencil. Beginning at the pocket top, sew down each line to create separations in the pocket panel, using decorative or straight stitching, as desired. Backstitch at the very top and bottom to keep the pockets strong and secure. Finish the pocket by topstitching across the bottom length to close the bottom of the pockets.

4. Pin the 2 lining pieces right sides together and sew along the sides and bottom, leaving about 4″ open along the center of the bottom for turning. Box the corners as in Step 8 in Bag Exterior (page 68). Press.

HANDLES AND SWIVEL SNAP

Adjust the handle length to suit your personal preference. The average handle is 24″ long end-to-end, creating a 12″ drop.

1. Turn under ¼″ of one long side of the handle fabric piece and press. Place the pressed edge close to the edge of the cotton webbing and topstitch.

2. On an ironing board, turn the second raw edge under to align with the webbing edge, pressing as you go.

3. Topstitch down the second length of the handle. Repeat Steps 1 and 2 with the second handle.

4. Place the 2 handle straps together and make sure they are the same length. Trim as needed.

5. Place the end of a handle on the bag exterior front, right sides together, 2″ from the side seam. Pin, aligning the end of the handle with the raw edge at the top of the bag. Pin the other end of the handle in the same manner. Repeat for the second handle on the bag exterior back.

6. Before sewing, turn the pinned handles up, as if you were carrying the finished bag, to be sure they aren't twisted.

7. Stitch the handle ends to the bag, using a ¼″ seam allowance. Reinforce this stress area by stitching several times.

8. For the swivel latch, sew the 1½″ × 6″ piece into a tube, using a ¼″ seam allowance; turn. Put the fabric tube through the end of the swivel latch and fold the fabric tube in half. Stitch the tube close to the end of the latch to secure.

9. Align and pin the raw edges of the swivel latch fabric tube to the raw edges at the top of the right side of the bag exterior front, next to one of the handles. Stitch securely, using a ¼″ seam allowance.

FINISHING

1. Turn the bag exterior right side in, and place the handles and swivel latch *inside*.

2. Turn the bag lining right side out and place it inside the exterior, right sides together. Match the snap centers to the centers of the sides of the exterior and match the lining side seams to the exterior side seams. Pin.

3. Sew along the top edge. Double or triple stitch over the handles for reinforcement.

4. Turn the bag through the opening in the bottom seam of the lining. Smooth and adjust the lining. Press. Stitch closed the opening in the lining. Press again.

Pebble Stack Wallhanging

A simple stack of stones against a dreamy sand-and-sea background evokes memories of a lovely day at the shore. Use hand-painted or hand-dyed fabrics or batiks to create an organic, natural look.

FINISHED SIZE: 8½″ × 20½″

ARTIST: Deborah O'Hare

WEBSITES: quiltroutes.co.uk
quiltroutes.blogspot.com
thebluehare.blogspot.com
flickr.com/photos/quiltroutes/
quiltroutes.etsy.com
folksy.com/shops/thebluehare

Deborah O'Hare is a fabric painter and art quilt designer who creates unique hand-painted fabric and kits, which she sells through her business, Quilt Routes. Her designs reflect, among other things, the coastline and countryside of the Heritage Coast in South Wales, United Kingdom, where she lives. Visit her blog for tutorials on how to paint your own fabric for this and other projects.

Materials and Supplies

- Scraps for the pebbles in a variety of colors, such as sand, gray, and rust: largest scrap must be at least 2½″ × 5″

- Light blue fabric for the sky: ¼ yard

- Darker blue fabric for the sea: ¼ yard

- Light tan fabric for the sand: ¼ yard

- Slightly darker tan fabric for the sand: ¼ yard

- Binding: will be pieced from background fabric scraps

- Backing and hanging sleeve fabric: ⅜ yard

- Fusible web (17″ wide): ¼ yard

- Batting: 10″ × 22″

- Embroidery floss to contrast with pebbles

Cutting

Cut background fabrics so that any pattern is in a horizontal direction.

LIGHT BLUE FABRIC
Cut 1 rectangle 8½″ × 5″.

DARK BLUE FABRIC
Cut 1 rectangle 8½″ × 4½″.

LIGHT TAN FABRIC
Cut 1 rectangle 8½″ × 5″.

DARKER TAN FABRIC
Cut 1 rectangle 8½″ × 7½″.

LEFTOVER SKY AND SAND FABRICS
Cut rectangles 2½″ wide and varying from 1″ to 3″ in length for double-fold binding.

Instructions

All seam allowances are ¼".

1. Trace the pebble patterns (page 75) onto fusible web. Place these on the wrong side of various pebble fabrics, choosing the colors you like for each pebble. Fuse, following the manufacturer's instructions, and cut out.

2. Arrange the background pieces as in the photo (right), and stitch them together in order. Press.

3. Arrange the pebbles to your liking and fuse them to the background. Hand stitch them down with contrasting embroidery floss, using a small backstitch. For stitch information, see Embroidery Stitches (page 127).

4. Layer and baste the top, batting, and backing using your preferred method.

5. Machine quilt as desired, referring to the photos (page 72 and right) for ideas. In the quilt shown, which uses monofilament thread, the background was quilted with a variety of horizontal and zigzag lines to create movement.

6. Piece together the small 2½"-wide rectangles to make the binding. Sew it on using your preferred method. Note that Deborah matched the binding to each section of the background.

7. Add a hanging sleeve if desired.

Pebble patterns: Cut 1 of each.

Hermit Crab Stuffie

FINISHED SIZE: Approximately 7″ × 9″

This plaid-clad hermit crab is way too handsome to stay hidden inside his shell house. Make this striking and unusual soft sculpture, and *learn a little crustacean anatomy at the same time!*

ARTIST: Catherine L. Owen

WEBSITES: raggyrat.co.uk
raggyrat.blogspot.com

Humor and fun are a must. Catherine Owen's soft sculptures do all the naughty things she is not allowed to do, romping through their lives in one big adventure. She has a degree from the Edinburgh College of Art and is self-taught in many media, including painting and pottery. But she always comes back to fabric, including collage, machine embroidery, and hand embellishments. Catherine enjoys accepting challenges, which have inspired her to make a lobster costume and a 2-foot-long cuttlefish puppet!

Materials and Supplies

- Wool or mixed-fiber plaid fabric: at least 22″ × 24″
- Embroidery floss or crewel wool in a complementary color
- Neoprene sheet, 1mm thick, such as Funky Foam* (not adhesive backed), for the carapace (shell): approximately 5″ × 8″
- Round, hollow plastic cording, such as Scoubidou,* for the antennae: about 14″
- ⅜″ shank buttons for eyes: 2
- Fiberfill stuffing for filling the body, claws, and legs
- Plastic pellets or rice for filling the abdomen
- Doll needle
  * *Available in craft stores and online*

Cutting

PLASTIC CORDING

Cut 2 pieces 2½″ long.

Cut 2 pieces 4½″ long.

Instructions

Template patterns are on pages 124 and 125. Patterns do not include seam allowances. Cut all plaid pieces on the bias, except for the 2 eyestalks.

CARAPACE, ABDOMEN, AND BODY

1. Cut 2 carapace (shell) pieces from the neoprene sheet. Cut 1 carapace piece from wool plaid, adding a ¼″ seam allowance for turning under the edges. Cut 2 body pieces, adding a ¼″ seam allowance. Fold a piece of the remaining wool diagonally. Place the abdomen pattern along the fold and cut out, adding a ¼″ seam allowance to all sides except the fold side.

2. Layer the neoprene pieces and machine stitch them together. Use a wide, long zigzag stitch and bring the edges together as you sew (practice on a scrap first). Alternatively, use dots of hot glue.

3. Place the wool carapace over the layered neoprene. You can secure it with pushpins, but watch out for the sharp points! Hand stitch the fabric to the foam, using embroidery floss and a blanket stitch; fold under the edges of the wool as you go. For stitch information, see Embroidery Stitches (page 127).

4. To make the abdomen from the folded wool, sew only the long, curved edge, leaving it open where indicated. Open the wool up into a tube, then squash it flat at the tail end. Sew across to close the tail end. Leave the body end open. Turn the abdomen right side out.

5. To make the body, pin and sew together the 2 body pieces, leaving it open where indicated. Carefully make a 1½″ slit in the middle of one piece; this slit will later be covered by the carapace.

6. With the slit on the body and the opening on the abdomen facing up, insert the abdomen through the slit on the body, open-edge first, and align the open end of the abdomen with the opening at the back of the body. Scrunch up the abdomen opening to make it fit. Pin and sew closed. Go over the seam again to make it secure.

7. Turn right side out and stuff the body firmly. Hand stitch the slit closed.

EYES

1. Cut out the eyestalk strips on the straight grain of the wool. Starting at a short end, roll it up tightly and pin. With embroidery floss, sew down the end using a few blanket stitches. Make 2 eyestalks.

2. Thread a needle with strong thread, knotted at one end. Referring to the photo (page 76) for placement, insert the needle in the top of the head, coming out in the middle of an eye position.

3. Pull the thread through the middle of an eyestalk, through a shank button, and back through the stalk and the head.

4. Make small stitches on top of the crab to secure; all will be hidden under the carapace later.

5. Repeat Steps 2–4 for the second eye.

ANTENNAE

1. For the first short antenna: Thread a doll needle with embroidery floss, and thread it through a hollow 2½″ plastic cording strand, leaving 1″ of thread sticking out of the end.

2. Tie a knot in the cording about ½″ from the loose end, securing the thread inside the cording. Push the needle into the head close to an eye, and pull it through to the top of the head, making small stitches to secure it.

3. Repeat Steps 1 and 2 for the second short antenna, placing it close to the other eye.

4. Make the long antennae in a similar way, except tie the knot ½″ from the other end to create an angle. Attach the antennae as in Step 2.

LEGS AND CLAWS

A hermit crab has 2 arms with claws—one slightly bigger than the other—2 pairs of walking legs, and 2 pairs of "reduced" legs that it uses to grip the inside of its shell "house."

1. Cut out 2 pieces of wool for the right claw, adding a ¼″ seam allowance. Layer the 2 wool pieces right sides together. Trace the pattern and either pin it to the 2 pieces and sew around it or draw around it and stitch on the lines. Remember to leave the indicated edge open for turning and stuffing.

2. Clip the seam allowance at the joints. Turn right side out.

3. Repeat Steps 1 and 2 for the left claw, the 4 walking legs, and the 4 reduced legs. For the reduced legs, clip the inner curve before turning right side out. (It can be tricky to turn the smaller legs. A small hemostat or tweezers can help.)

4. Once the claws are right side out, cut the slit and small triangle (drawn on the pattern) for the pincers. Using embroidery floss and a blanket stitch, sew these cut edges together to mimic the pincers' serrated edges.

5. Stuff each pincer of each claw, stopping just before the first joint. Squash the arm flat and topstitch across to create a joint. (Use a sewing machine fitted with a zipper foot to get close to the stuffed section, or just take a few neat hand stitches.)

6. Stuff the middle section of each claw, but this time push the seams together before sewing across the joint.

7. Fold in the seam allowance of the opening and stuff the last segment of each arm. Close the arms with a gathering stitch before sewing them to the body with a ladder stitch. Refer to the photo (page 76) for placement, remembering that most hermit crabs have the arm with the largest claw on the right.

8. For each walking leg, stuff the curved tip before squashing the seams together and sewing across the joint, as you did for the arms. Stuff the middle section; then squash the seams together and again sew across the joint.

9. Fold in the seam allowance of the opening and stuff the last segment, closing the leg with a gathering stitch before sewing it to the body with a ladder stitch. Refer to the photo (page 76) to attach all 4 walking legs to the crab's underside, making sure that the curved tips point down and the legs curl under the body.

10. Do not stuff the reduced legs. Just fold in the tops and sew them closed before ladder stitching them to the body. Position them so they curl under the body.

CRAB ASSEMBLY

1. Use 2 pins to hold the carapace in position on the crab's back. Use strong thread and a ladder stitch to attach it, pulling the thread through the body along the seam and through the carapace on the underside only, level with the bottom of the blanket stitch.

2. Carefully fill the abdomen with plastic pellets or rice. Do not overfill; leave a bit of space for the abdomen to squash down so you can place it in a shell or other "home." Close the seam with small ladder stitches.

Sand and Surf Bag

Hit the sand with all your gear stowed in this roomy bag that sports zippered pockets galore, a drawstring closure, an adjustable shoulder strap, and a carrying handle—the works! Make it in bold red, as shown here, or whatever color strikes your fancy.

FINISHED SIZE: 6″ tall (folded); 24″ tall (unfolded); 13″ bottom diameter

ARTIST: Anita Peluso

WEBSITES: bloominworkshop.com
bloominworkshop.wordpress.com

Through her business, Bloomin' Workshop, Anita Peluso designs quilt patterns that are primarily sold through a local quilt shop and distributed by a local fabric manufacturer. Between designing and making quilts, she teaches beginning quilting techniques and blogs about her quilting adventures.

Materials and Supplies

- Canvas or heavyweight fabric (at least 54″ wide): 1½ yards
- Lining and bag accent fabric (44″ wide): 1½ yards
- 9″ nonseparating, plastic molded-teeth zippers: 3
- 2″ slider and 2″ loop for adjustable shoulder strap
- Paper-backed fusible web: 5″ × 6″

Cutting

CANVAS

Cut a 14″-diameter circle for the bag bottom.

Cut 2 rectangles 21⅜″ × 25″ for the bag body.

Cut 2 rectangles 2½″ × 10½″ for the side pocket upper pieces.

Cut 2 rectangles 7″ × 10½″ for the side pocket lower pieces.

Cut 1 rectangle 2″ × 10½″ for the top pocket upper piece.

Cut 1 rectangle 6″ × 10½″ for the top pocket lower piece.

Cut 1 strip 6″ × width of fabric for the shoulder strap and handle.

Cut 1 rectangle 4″ × 10½″ for the handle support.

Cut 2 strips 3″ × width of fabric for the drawstring ties and loops.

LINING FABRIC

Cut a 14″-diameter circle for the bag bottom.

Cut 2 rectangles 21⅜″ × 25″ for the bag sides.

Cut 2 rectangles 3½″ × 21⅜″ for the accent stripes.

Cut 1 piece 5″ × 6″ for the crab appliqué.

Instructions

Note: All seam allowances are ½".

SIDE POCKETS

Note: One pocket zipper opens to the left, and the other zipper opens to the right.

1. Zigzag, serge, or otherwise finish all the edges of the pocket pieces.

2. Turn under a 10½" edge of the pocket upper pieces ½"; press.

3. Center the folded edge of each pocket piece on top of an open zipper, pin, and topstitch ⅛" from the folded edge. Place 1 zipper with its tab on the right of the upper piece and the other with its tab to the left. That way 1 zipper will open to the left and the other to the right. Add a second line of top stitching ¼" away from the first.

4. Repeat Steps 2 and 3 to stitch the lower side pocket pieces to the other side of the zipper.

5. Turn under the top and side edges of each pocket ½"; press.

6. Fold each pocket vertically to find the center; mark. Mark the center of each bag body along the 21⅜" edge. Place the pockets right side up on top of the right side of the bag body pieces, aligning the bottom edges and matching the center marks.

7. Double topstitch around the sides and top edge of each pocket, as in Step 3.

ACCENT STRIPE

1. Turn under the 21⅜″ edges of the 2 bag accent stripe pieces ½″; press.

2. Pin the accent stripes directly above the pockets on the 2 bag body pieces and topstitch in place ⅛″ away from the folded edge.

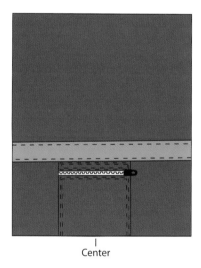

Center

3. Place the 2 body pieces right sides together and sew the back seam of the bag.

4. Press the seam to one side and double topstitch the seam.

TOP POCKET

1. Follow Steps 1–4 from Side Pockets (page 84).

2. Trace the crab appliqué pattern (page 124) and cut out a template. Trace it on the paper side of the fusible web. Follow the manufacturer's directions to fuse it to the wrong side of the 5″ × 6″ lining fabric. Cut out the shape.

3. Center the crab on the bottom half of the top pocket, and fuse. Machine stitch around the crab twice. Machine or hand sew the eyes using thread in an accent color.

4. Turn under the pocket top and sides ½″. Press. Mark the center, and place the pocket on the bag body, aligning the bottom edges and matching the center mark with the center back seam.

5. Double topstitch around the pocket sides and top edges.

Bottom

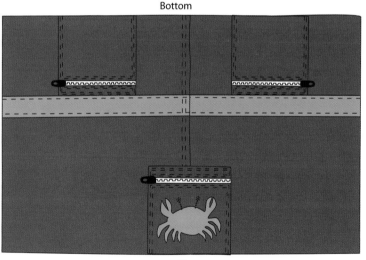

Top

SHOULDER STRAP

1. Turn under 2″ along a long edge of the 6″ × width of fabric strip for the strap; press.

2. Turn under the other long edge ½″; press. Fold this edge again along the raw edge of the first folded edge and press. It will overlap just to the center of the strap, not all the way to the first fold.

3. Topstitch ⅛″ away from the centered folded edge. Add a second line of topstitching ½″ from the first.

4. From the finished strap, cut a 3″-long piece for the tab at the bottom of the shoulder strap, a 10″-long piece for the handle at the top of the bag, and at least 36″ (or desired length) for the adjustable shoulder strap.

5. Attach the 2″ slider to an end of the 36″ shoulder strap piece. Fold under the end, and topstitch to create a loop holding the slider.

6. Fold the 3″ tab in half, and place the 2″ plastic loop inside the fold to create the bottom tab of the adjustable shoulder strap.

7. Thread the strap through the slider as shown.

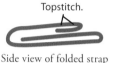

Topstitch.

Side view of folded strap

Top view of folded strap

Loop

Tab

Bottom of bag

Slider

Top of bag

Topstitch.

DRAWSTRING TIES AND LOOPS

1. Trim the selvage from one end of each 3″ × width of fabric strip for the drawstring ties. Turn under ½″. Press. Topstitch. This will be the finished end of the tie.

2. On each strip, turn under ¼″ along one long edge and ¾″ along the other long edge. Fold the strip in half and topstitch ⅛″ from the folded edge, as shown.

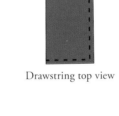

Topstitch.
Drawstring side view

Drawstring top view

3. Cut each strip into 1 piece 30″ long and 2 pieces 4″ long, for a total of 2 ties 30″ long and 4 loops 4″ long. Make sure the 30″ pieces are measured from the finished edge of each strip.

BAG AND LINING ASSEMBLY

1. Fold the bag in half, right sides together, and sew the front seam of the bag. Press the seam to one side and double topstitch the seam.

2. Center the folded shoulder strap tab on the back bottom edge of the bag body over the back seam; pin.

3. Fold the 14″-diameter circle for the bag bottom in half and mark the center of the fold on each edge.

4. Match the fold marks with the seams at the front and back of the bag body and pin in place all the way around, right sides together. Sew the bag bottom to the bag body, catching the edges of the loop tab in the seam.

5. Place the 2 lining fabric bag sides right sides together. Sew the front and back seam along the 25″ edges.

6. Fold and mark the circle for the lining bottom as for the bag in Step 3. Sew the lining bottom to the lining body as for the bag in Step 4.

7. With the bag inside out and the lining right side out, place the lining inside the bag, with the right sides of the bag and the lining facing each other.

8. Sew the bag and lining together around the top, leaving a 5″–6″ opening for turning.

9. Turn the bag right side out and push the lining into the bag.

10. Press the edge of the bag and sew the opening closed. Double topstitch the edge.

STRAP, HANDLE, AND TIES

1. On the 4″ × 10½″ handle support piece, turn under 1″ along both 10½″ edges. Then turn under ½″ on each end.

2. Place the support ¾″ below the top edge of the bag top pocket, and pin through the bag and lining.

3. Pin the cut ends of the 30″-long ties under each end of the handle support.

4. Pin the end of the adjustable shoulder strap under the center of the handle support.

5. Double topstitch around the edge of the handle support, through all the layers of the ties and shoulder strap.

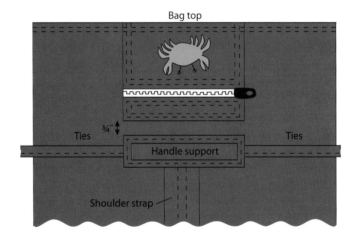

6. On the 10″ handle piece from Step 4 of Shoulder Strap (page 86) fold under each end ½″; press.

7. Pin the handle ends onto the handle support ¾″ from each end of the handle support. Topstitch the handle ends ⅛″ from the folded edge. Trim the folded-under raw edges close to the stitching.

8. Topstitch ¼″ from the first line of topstitching toward the center to enclose the handle's trimmed raw edges.

9. To mark the loop positions, measure 6″ from one end of the bag handle support; mark. Measure another 6″ and mark again.

10. Measuring from the other end of the bag handle support, repeat Step 9.

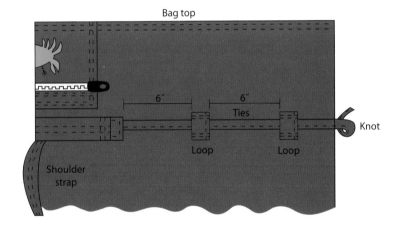

11. Turn under ½″ on each end of the 4″ loop pieces; press.

12. Pin the loops in place over the marks from the bag handle, and double topstitch the loops to the bag and through the lining layer. Trim any excess fabric from the loop edges.

13. Feed the ties through the loops toward the front of the bag, and knot the ends.

Porthole Baby Quilt

FINISHED SIZE: 42" × 42"

This special quilt with a porthole of jolly prints in beach-towel bright colors will make playtime on the sand fun for the little ones. When the sun sets, shake it out, wash it up, and it's ready for your next family outing.

ARTIST: Latifah Saafir

WEBSITES: thequiltengineer.com
flickr.com/photos/latifahsaafir
thequiltengineer.etsy.com

Sewing has been Latifah Saafir's portal to creativity ever since—at age six—she learned to sew at her mother's knee. Latifah focused on sewing garments through her teenage years and college. A mechanical engineer by training, she took design classes "to keep her sanity." She discovered quilting in 2009, immediately co-founded the Modern Quilt Guild, and created more than 20 quilts in her first year. Latifah is known for her bold use of color and innovative design. She is excited to be working on her first series of quilt patterns and products.

Materials and Supplies

- Blue fabrics: a variety to total ½ yard or 40 squares 3½″ × 3½″
- Orange fabrics: a variety to total ½ yard or 35 squares 3½″ × 3½″
- Yellow fabrics: a variety to total ½ yard or 35 squares 3½″ × 3½″
- Brown fabrics: a variety to total ½ yard or 35 squares 3½″ × 3½″
- Brown solid fabric: 1¼ yards for the "porthole" ring
- Aqua blue solid fabric: 1⅓ yards* for the background
- Batting: 45″ × 45″
- Backing fabric: 1⅓ yards**
- Binding fabric: ¾ yard
- Freezer paper (18″ wide): 3⅞ yards
- Poster board or other rigid paper: 1 strip 22″ × 2″
- Pushpin
- Fine-tip marker
- Gluestick

    * Requires a 40½″ usable fabric width

    ** Requires a 45″ fabric width with a 42″ usable width

Cutting

BLUE FABRICS
Cut 40 squares 3½″ × 3½″.

ORANGE, YELLOW, AND BROWN FABRICS
From *each*, cut 35 squares 3½″ × 3½″.

BINDING FABRIC
Cut 5 strips 4½″ × width of fabric for double-fold binding.

FREEZER PAPER
Cut 3 panels 45″ × width of freezer paper.

Instructions

Note: All seam allowances are ¼".

BLOCK UNIT FOR THE CENTER CIRCLE

1. Arrange and sew together all 145 blue, orange, brown, and yellow squares into 13 rows, with the following number of squares in each row:

Row 1: 7 squares   Row 11: 11 squares
Row 2: 9 squares   Row 12: 9 squares
Row 3: 11 squares   Row 13: 7 squares
Rows 4–10: 13 squares each

   Press the seams open.

2. Sew together the rows; press the seams open.

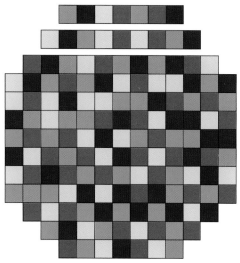

Block unit assembly diagram

QUILT TOP ASSEMBLY

1. Tape together the long sides of the freezer paper sheets. Fold the joined sheets in half lengthwise and across to locate the center, and mark it with an X.

2. To make a circle guide, mark a dot 1″ from one end of the poster board strip. Measure again from the end of the poster board strip, and mark a dot 18″ away (inner circle) and 20″ away (outer circle). With a pushpin, make a hole through each mark, large enough for your marker tip to fit through.

3. Insert the pushpin through the strip at the 1″ hole and into the center X on the freezer paper. This process is easier if you push the pin through the paper and anchor it into a surface like your cutting mat. Holding the pushpin in place, insert the pen through the 18″ hole. Make sure the poster board strip is fully extended; then draw the first circle onto the freezer paper. You may have to stop and rotate the paper. Take your time to draw an even circle.

4. Move the pen into the 20″ hole and repeat Step 3 to draw the outer circle.

5. Cut out the smaller inside circle and discard the center. Center the remaining freezer paper pattern, shiny side down, on the wrong side of the solid brown fabric. Press it in place with a dry iron.

6. Cut out the fabric on the inside of the circle, leaving at least a 1″ seam allowance. Clip the seam allowance at 1″ intervals to within ⅛″ of the pattern.

7. Apply glue to the freezer paper around the edge of the circle, and fold the clipped seam allowance over the edge of the pattern. Generously apply glue along the clipped seam allowance.

8. Place the glued side of the fabric on the right side of the block unit for the center circle. Adjust to make sure the pattern is centered. Finger-press into place. Turn it over and use a dry iron on the back until the glue is dry.

9. Remove the freezer paper pattern from the fabric. Be careful not to tear the pattern because you will use it for the second circle. Set the pattern aside. Press the fabric again, so the clipped seam allowance has a crisp crease.

10. Without disturbing the glued-on seam allowance, gently unfold the circle fabric so you can sew on the wrong side of it. The circle fabric and the center block unit should be right sides together. Attach an open-toed or zipper foot to your sewing machine. With the clipped seam on top and extending to the right of the needle, sew just to the right of the pressed crease.

11. Releasing the glue, trim the seam to ¼″. Using steam, iron the seam allowance away from the center block unit.

12. Cut the freezer paper along the outer circle line and discard the center ring portion. Place the remaining freezer paper pattern, shiny side down, on the wrong side of the aqua blue background fabric. Press it in place with a dry iron.

13. Repeat Steps 6–11 to complete the quilt top.

14. Trim the quilt top to 40½″ × 40½″.

QUILTING AND FINISHING

1. Mark quilting designs as desired on the quilt top or plan to stitch without marking.

2. Layer and baste the quilt using your preferred method.

3. Quilt by hand or machine. Do not trim the batting and backing even with the quilt top. Trim the batting and backing to 42″ × 42″.

4. Bind the quilt using your preferred method. By aligning the raw edges of the binding with the raw edge of the quilt top and using a ¼″ seam allowance, the 4½″ strips will yield a 1″-wide finished binding.

Porthole Beach Ball

FINISHED SIZE: 8″ diameter

Make this soft, bouncy ball as a companion to the Porthole Baby Quilt (page 90) or on its own. Either way, it's great to toss around on the beach or in the backyard.

ARTIST: Latifah Saafir

WEBSITES: thequiltengineer.com
flickr.com/photos/latifahsaafir
thequiltengineer.etsy.com

For more about Latifah, see
her artist bio (page 91).

Materials and Supplies

- 2 different green fabrics:
  at least 5″ × 10″ each

- 2 different orange fabrics:
  at least 5″ × 10″ each

- 2 different yellow fabrics:
  at least 5″ × 10″ each

- 6 different brown fabrics:
  at least 3″ × 4″ each

- Fiberfill stuffing

Instructions

Note: All seam allowances are ¼″.

1. Trace the patterns (page 125) and cut out the templates. Using Template A, cut 1 each of the green, orange, and yellow fabrics, for a total of 6. Using Template B, cut 2 of each brown fabric, for a total of 12.

2. Create 6 panels by sewing a B piece to each end of the A pieces. Press the seams toward A.

3. Arrange the panels in an order that looks pleasing. Sew together 3 panels; then sew together the remaining 3 panels.

4. With right sides facing, sew together the 2 sets of panels made in Step 3. Leave a 3″ opening for turning.

5. Turn the ball right side out; stuff, filling it evenly and not too full. Whipstitch the opening closed.

Three Wish Fish

FINISHED FISH SIZE: 6¼″ long × 2½″ wide
FINISHED PROJECT SIZE: About 12″ × 12″

A colorful catch from a sea of modern graphic prints dangles porch-side in the breeze. You can stitch up a whole school of these fanciful, super-simple fish in no time.

ARTIST: Havilah Savage

WEBSITES: darlingsavage.com
darlingsavage.etsy.com
flickr.com/photos/32010457@N06/

Havilah Savage started her business, Darling Savage, in 2006 as a way to integrate her creative skills into the growing indie craft movement of Portland, Oregon. After participating for a couple of years in local craft shows, she opened her Etsy shop. Learning to run her own business has been a wonderful, exciting experience. She adores trying out original project ideas, often incorporating fun embellishments and vintage objects. Havilah's soft goods are all designed using a blend of repurposed, vintage, and new fabrics and materials. She scours local thrift shops for quality fabrics and designs her sewing projects to create as little waste as possible. Darling Savage is committed to environmental sustainability and uses 95 percent natural, renewable, and/or recycled materials in each project.

Materials and Supplies

- 3 different fabrics: at least 6″ × 7″ each
- Buttons (4-hole style, about ½″): 3
- Fiberfill or natural bamboo stuffing
- Jute or sisal twine,* about ¼″ thick: 25″
- Sturdy twig: approximately 12″–15″ long
- Thread
- Crafter's glue (optional)

If you can't find thick twine, braid together 3 lengths of thinner twine.

Instructions

All seam allowances are ¼″.

1. Trace the pattern (page 101), and cut out a template. Cut 2 (a front and a back) from each fabric.

2. Sew a button to one side of each fish, for eyes. (Use 4-hole buttons and crisscross the stitches.)

3. Place the fish fronts and backs *wrong* sides together. Sew around the body and across the end before the tail, leaving an opening for stuffing. Stuff the fish with fiberfill and hand stitch the opening closed. Leave the tail unstitched and the fabric edges unfinished.

4. Attach the fish to the twig with a needle and thread, wrapping the thread 3 or 4 times around the twig. Tie off and clip the loose thread ends.

5. For the hanger, tie the ends of the twine around either end of the twig. You may wish to secure the twine with a dab of crafter's glue.

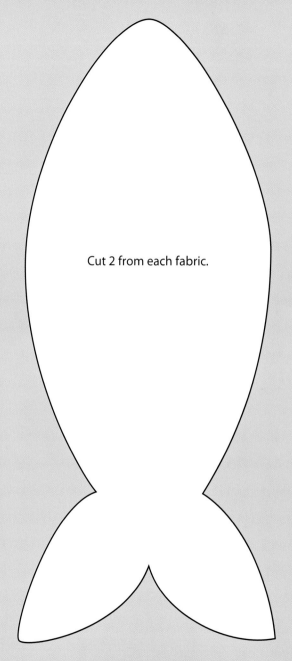

Cut 2 from each fabric.

Three Wish Fish pattern

Anchors Away Felt Banner

A jaunty red, white, and blue banner festooned across a window, doorway, or shelf lends nautical style to any occasion, from a child's party to a Fourth of July bash. Or use it anytime to perk up your decor.

FINISHED FLAG SIZE: 4½″ × 6″
FINISHED BANNER SIZE: Approximately 60″ long

ARTISTS: Angela J. & Kristina K., owners of Taffie Wishes

WEBSITES: taffiewishes.etsy.com
taffiewishes.blogspot.com

Kristina and Angela are stay-at-home mom friends who came up with the idea to start their business, Taffie Wishes, while planning their children's birthday parties. Store-bought decorations didn't have the innocence and simplicity they were looking for. They wanted to create party decorations that both children and parents would love—and that after the party could be used as decor for nurseries or kids' bedrooms. Their first products went up for sale in their Etsy shop in June 2010, and they have experienced steady growth since then. They look forward to even more opportunities in the future!

Materials and Supplies

- Felt sheets (9″ × 12″), such as Eco-fi felt: 1 red, 1 white, 2 navy blue, and 2 cadet blue for flags and appliqués
- Embroidery floss: 1 skein each of white, blue, and red
- ¾″ red button: 1 for ship's wheel
- ½″ red buttons: 8 for sailboats
- ½″ white buttons: 2 for anchors
- White ⅛″ upholstery cord: 6 yards
- Paper-backed fusible web, such as Heat*n*Bond Ultra Hold (17″ wide): ½ yard
- Embroidery needle

Cutting

FELT SHEETS

Cut cadet blue and navy blue sheets in half crosswise to make 8 pieces 4½″ × 12″.

PAPER-BACKED FUSIBLE WEB

Cut 7 pieces 4½″ × 4¾″.

Instructions

Makes 7 flags.

MAKE THE FLAGS

Note: Sew appliqués onto the fronts of the flags only; backs are unembellished. For stitch information, see Embroidery Stitches (page 127).

1. Trace the patterns (page 107) and cut out templates. Cut 2 anchor pieces from the red felt. Cut 4 small sail pieces, 4 large sail pieces, and the ship's wheel circle from the white felt. Cut 4 boat pieces from a navy blue half-piece.

2. Fold 2 of the 4½″ × 12″ navy blue pieces in half to create 2 flags 4½″ × 6″. Center a red anchor on the front of each; pin. With white embroidery floss, use a whipstitch to stitch evenly around the entire anchor. Sew a white button onto each.

3. Fold the remaining 4½″ × 12″ navy blue piece in half to create another flag. Center the ship's wheel on the front; pin. With white floss, use a running stitch to stitch the wheel in place. Sew the large red button onto the center of the wheel.

4. Starting from the center button, sew a straight line of 4 even stitches outward to the white circle. Sew an additional 3 stitches outside of the circle. Leave ⅛″ of space; then sew stitches to match going back toward the button center. Continue in this fashion, creating 8 even sets of stitches. Refer to the photo (right) for stitch placement.

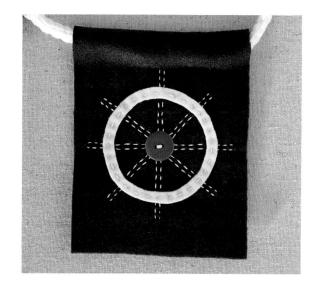

5. Fold the 4½″ × 12″ cadet blue pieces in half to create 4 flags. Place the navy blue boat pieces about ⅓ away from the bottom of each flag. Sew 2 small red buttons on each boat, using blue floss.

6. With blue floss and a running stitch, sew around the outside of each navy blue boat piece.

7. Place the large white sails on the flags, pinning if necessary. With blue floss, sew a running stitch from the boat up the left side of the sail. Near the top of the sail, stitch a single line.

8. With red floss, sew a double line of running stitches near the center of each large sail. With white floss, sew along the bottom edge of each.

9. Place the small white sails on the flags, touching the inside corners of the large sails. Using white floss, sew along the bottom and left side of each small sail piece. Use white floss to stitch "waves" under the sailboats.

ASSEMBLE THE BANNER

1. Cut the upholstery cord into 3 sections, each 6′ long. Tie them all together in a knot at one end. Braid them, and then tie a knot at the other end.

2. Following the manufacturer's instructions, use the fusible web to adhere the flag fronts and backs, wrong sides together, leaving an open channel at the tops for stringing onto the cord. *Note: Be very careful not to scorch the felt when ironing. Test on a scrap piece before working on the finished flags.*

3. String the flags onto the cord. If necessary, use a craft stick or a chopstick to help push the rope through the channel in each flag.

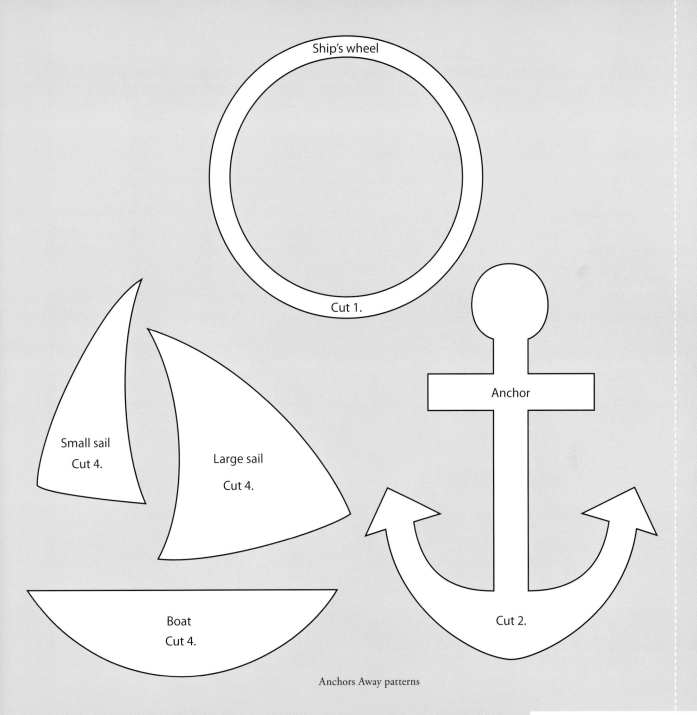

Ship's wheel

Cut 1.

Small sail
Cut 4.

Large sail
Cut 4.

Anchor

Cut 2.

Boat
Cut 4.

Anchors Away patterns

Beach Crab Pillow

FINISHED SIZE: *20″ × 20″*

*In a zigzag sea of blue and white, a spot of bright orange appears: It's
a little crab, scuttling across this plump, inviting pillow to add its own
colorful whimsy to this fresh, modern design.*

ARTIST: Heidi Troyer

WEBSITES: craftnosis.blogspot.com
ylheidi.etsy.com
flickr.com/photos/craftnosis/

Heidi Troyer is a prolific quilter with a passion for combining traditional quilt patterns and modern fabrics. Her love of textiles drew her into the online quilting community, which led to the creation of her own Etsy shop specializing in one-of-a-kind pillows. She shares her creative process and journey through her blog.

Materials and Supplies

- Aqua print fabrics: a variety to total ⅜ yard for half-square triangle units
- Ivory solid fabric: ⅝ yard for half-square triangle units and solid squares
- Orange print fabric 1: 6″ × 6½″ for the appliqué
- Orange print fabric 2: 2½″ × 4″ for the appliqué
- Backing fabric: ½ yard
- Binding fabric: ¼ yard
- Cotton batting: 22″ × 22″
- Paper-backed fusible web: ¼ yard
- 20″ pillow form

Cutting

AQUA PRINT FABRICS

Cut 60 squares 2½″ × 2½″ for half-square triangle units.

IVORY SOLID FABRIC

Cut 48 squares 2½″ × 2½″ for half-square triangle units.

Cut 36 squares 2⅛″ × 2⅛″ for the solid squares.

BACKING FABRIC

Cut 2 rectangles 15″ × 20″ for the pillow back.

BINDING FABRIC

Cut 3 strips 2½″ × width of fabric for the double-fold binding.

Instructions

Note: All seam allowances are ¼".

PILLOW FRONT ASSEMBLY

1. On the wrong side of an aqua 2½" × 2½" square, use a ruler and pencil to draw a diagonal line from corner to corner. Place this square right sides together with an aqua 2½" square of a different fabric. Sew ¼" from each side of the drawn line. Cut along the pencil line and press toward the darker fabric.

2. Repeat Step 1 to make a total of 12 aqua/aqua half-square triangle units.

3. Repeat Step 1 using ivory and aqua squares to make a total of 96 aqua/ivory half-square triangle units.

4. Lay out the half-square tri-angle units and the ivory 2⅛" × 2⅛" squares to form the pillow's zigzag pattern.

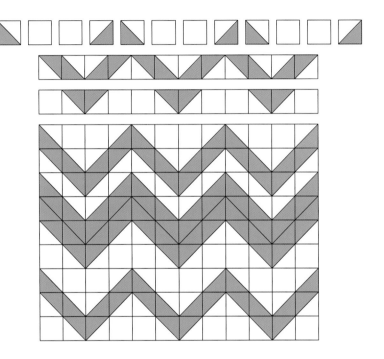

5. Sew the blocks together to form horizontal rows; press the seams open. Sew the rows together to form the pillow top; again, press the seams open.

6. Center the pillow front wrong side down on the batting square and baste.

7. Following the edge of each aqua "wave," stitch lines ¼" apart in the ivory sections.

8. Trim the batting even with the edges of the pillow front.

APPLIQUÉ

1. Trace the crab claws and center shell patterns (page 126) onto the paper side of the fusible web, and roughly cut out the shapes.

2. Follow the manufacturer's instructions to fuse the web to the wrong side of the orange fabrics. Cut out the pieces on the traced line.

3. Referring to the photo for placement, place the claws, then the center shell, on the top right corner of the pillow front. Press into place.

4. Topstitch around the body and the shell using white thread. For a more organic look, stitch around each shape twice.

FINISHING

1. Fold under 3″ of a long side of each 15″ × 20″ rectangle; press.

2. Layer the pillow front and the 2 backing rectangles with wrong sides together, raw edges aligned, and folded edges toward the center.

3. Bind the pillow together using your preferred method.

Patterns

Coquillages à la Plage:
A Seaside Garland

Project on page 10

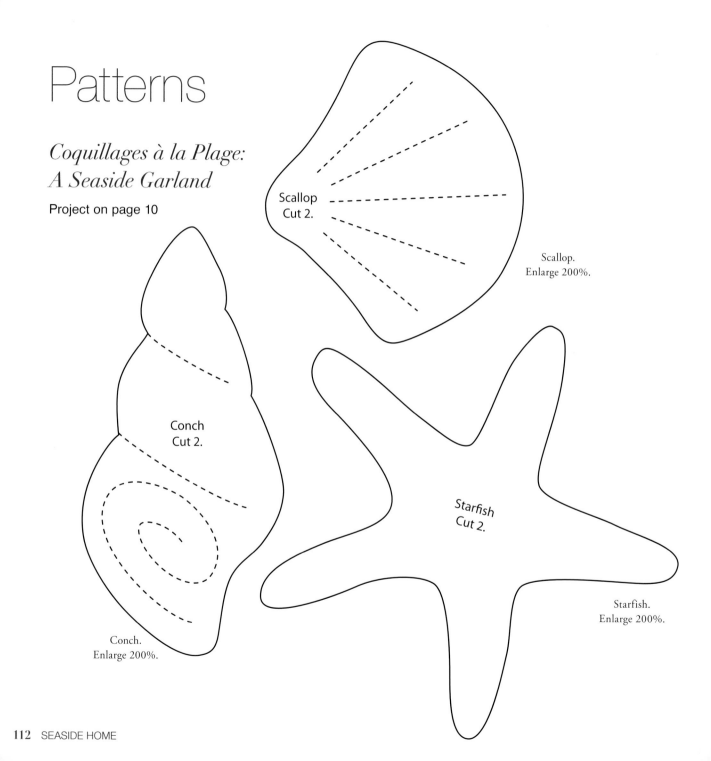

Scallop
Cut 2.

Scallop.
Enlarge 200%.

Conch
Cut 2.

Conch.
Enlarge 200%.

Starfish
Cut 2.

Starfish.
Enlarge 200%.

Fabric-Wrapped Wreath

Project on page 14

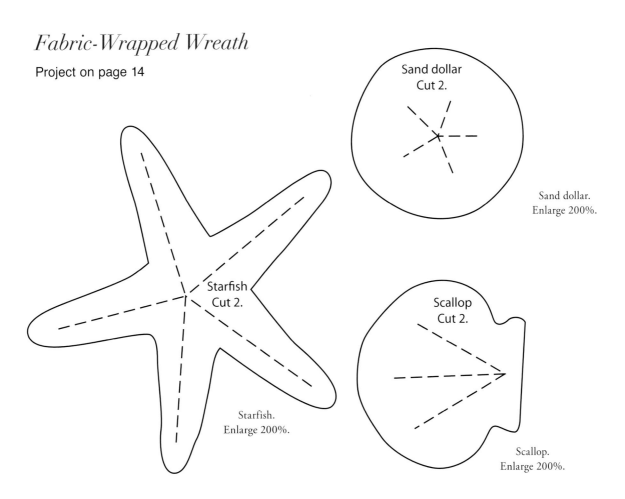

Sand dollar
Cut 2.

Sand dollar.
Enlarge 200%.

Starfish
Cut 2.

Starfish.
Enlarge 200%.

Scallop
Cut 2.

Scallop.
Enlarge 200%.

Sea Turtle Quilt

Project on page 18

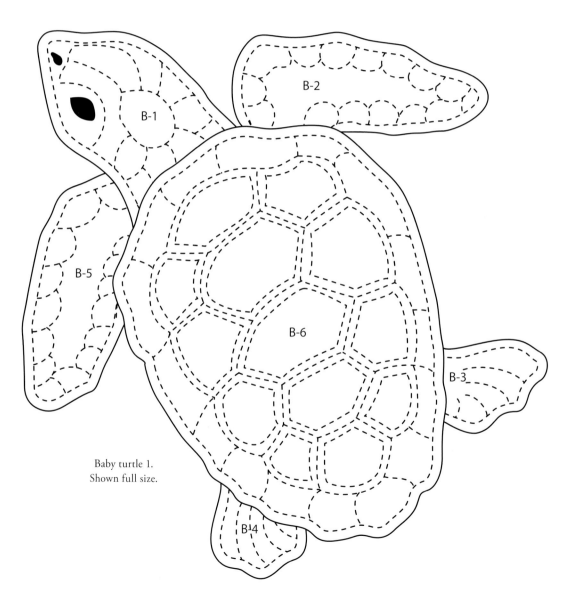

Baby turtle 1.
Shown full size.

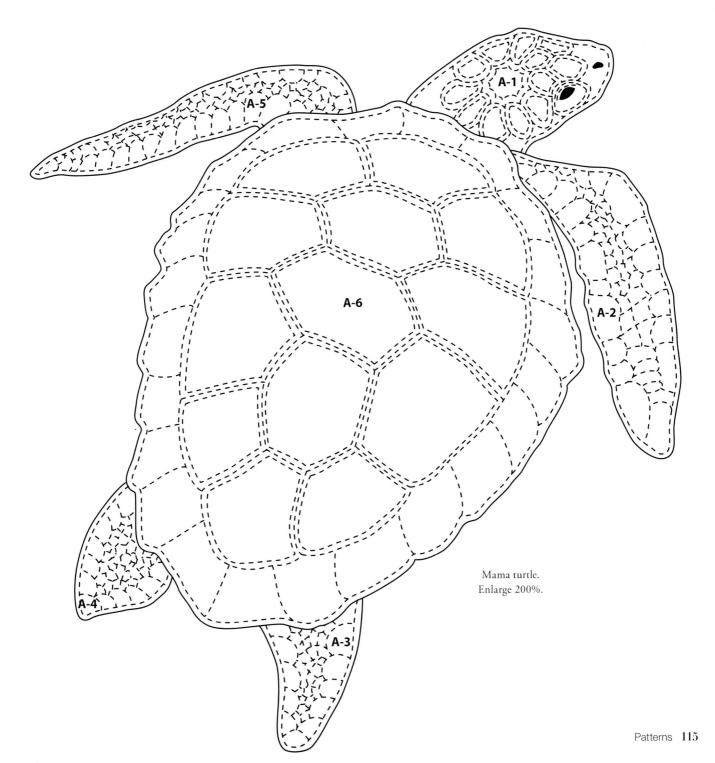

A-5

A-1

A-2

A-6

A-4

A-3

Mama turtle.
Enlarge 200%.

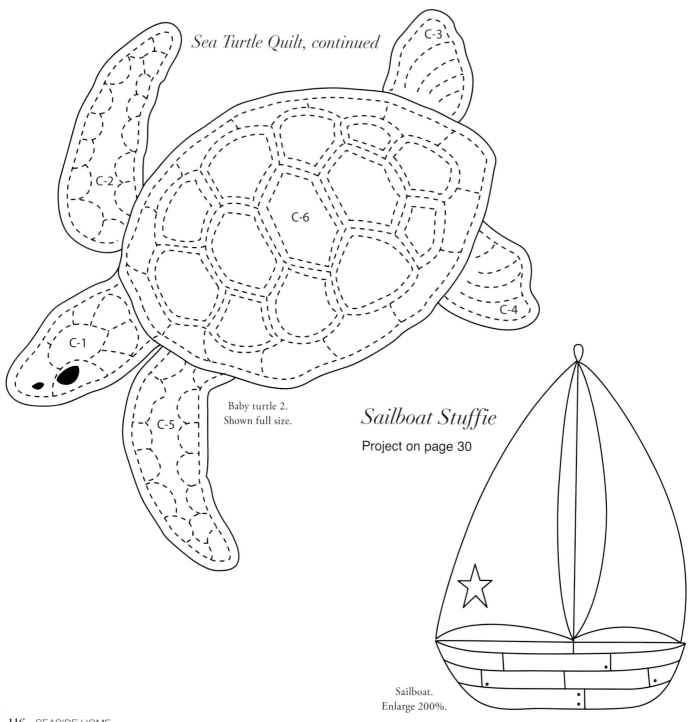

Sea Turtle Quilt, continued

C-3

C-2

C-6

C-1

Baby turtle 2.
Shown full size.

C-4

C-5

Sailboat Stuffie

Project on page 30

Sailboat.
Enlarge 200%.

Deep Waters Quilt

Project on page 32

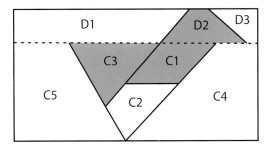

Bird block piecing pattern. Enlarge 200%.

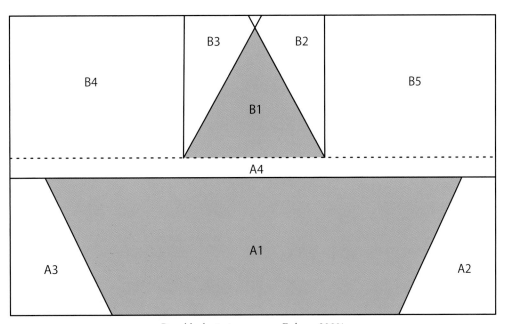

Boat block piecing pattern. Enlarge 200%.

Seashore Sunhat

Project on page 36

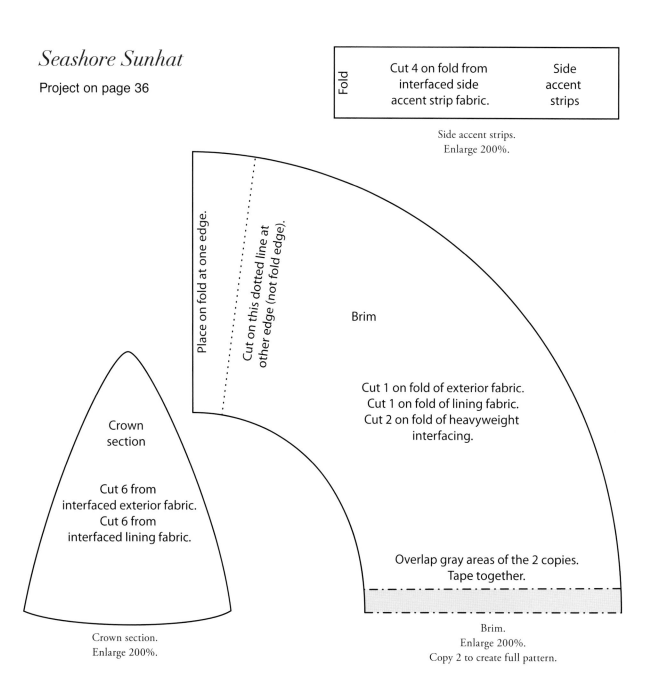

Cut 4 on fold from interfaced side accent strip fabric.

Side accent strips

Side accent strips.
Enlarge 200%.

Place on fold at one edge.

Cut on this dotted line at other edge (not fold edge).

Brim

Cut 1 on fold of exterior fabric.
Cut 1 on fold of lining fabric.
Cut 2 on fold of heavyweight interfacing.

Crown section

Cut 6 from interfaced exterior fabric.
Cut 6 from interfaced lining fabric.

Overlap gray areas of the 2 copies.
Tape together.

Crown section.
Enlarge 200%.

Brim.
Enlarge 200%.
Copy 2 to create full pattern.

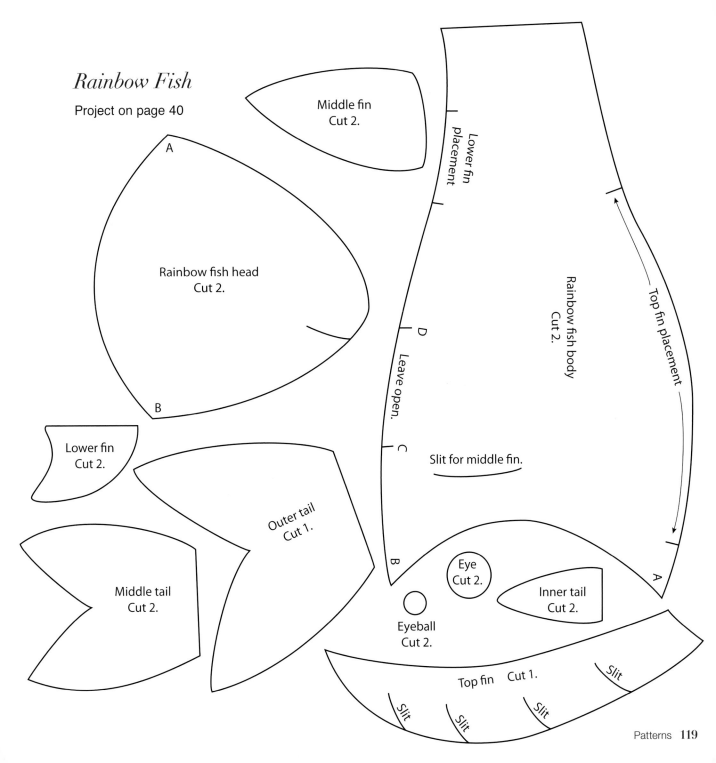

Rainbow Fish

Project on page 40

Middle fin
Cut 2.

Rainbow fish head
Cut 2.

A

B

Lower fin placement

Lower fin
Cut 2.

Top fin placement

Rainbow fish body
Cut 2.

D

Leave open.

C

Slit for middle fin.

Outer tail
Cut 1.

Middle tail
Cut 2.

B

Eye
Cut 2.

Inner tail
Cut 2.

A

Eyeball
Cut 2.

Top fin   Cut 1.

Slit

Slit

Slit

Slit

Slit

Sparkly Starfish

Project on page 44

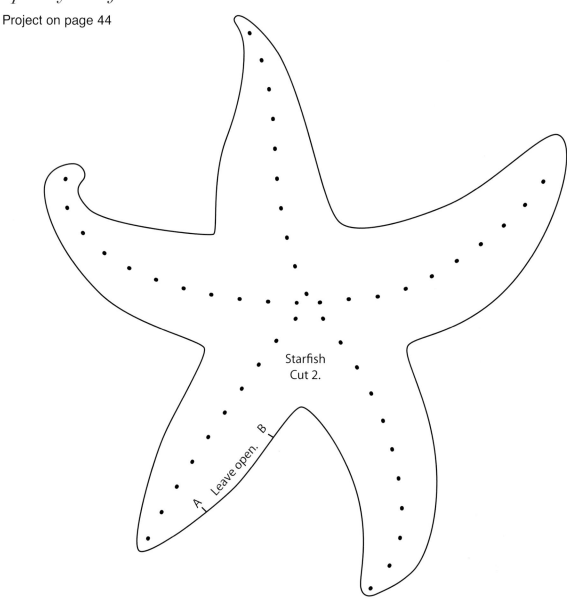

Starfish
Cut 2.

A | Leave open. B |

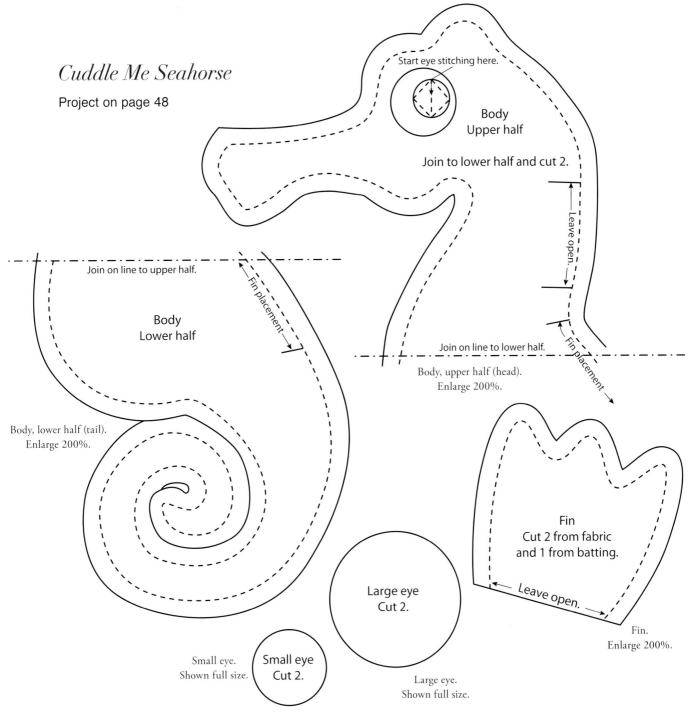

Cuddle Me Seahorse

Project on page 48

Start eye stitching here.

Body
Upper half

Join to lower half and cut 2.

Leave open.

Body, upper half (head).
Enlarge 200%.

Join on line to upper half.

Fin placement

Body
Lower half

Fin placement

Join on line to lower half.

Body, lower half (tail).
Enlarge 200%.

Fin
Cut 2 from fabric
and 1 from batting.

Leave open.

Fin.
Enlarge 200%.

Large eye
Cut 2.

Small eye.
Shown full size.

Small eye
Cut 2.

Large eye.
Shown full size.

Saucy Mermaid

Project on page 62

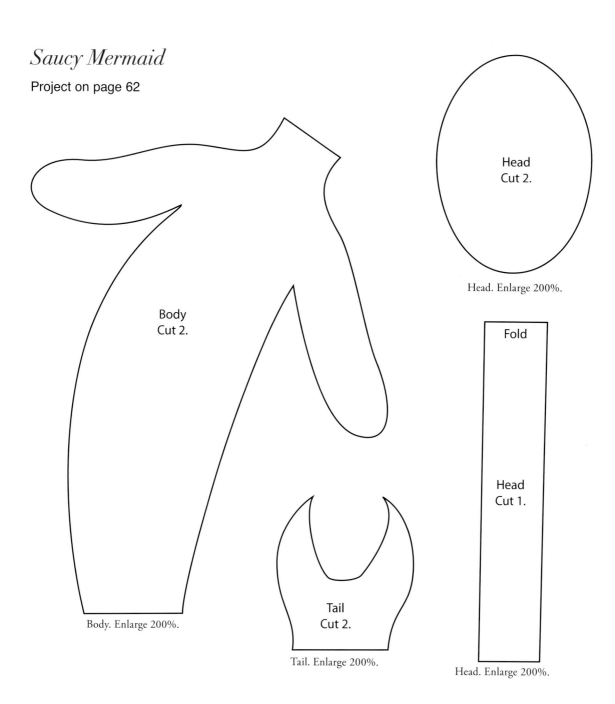

Body. Enlarge 200%.

Head. Enlarge 200%.

Tail. Enlarge 200%.

Head. Enlarge 200%.

Body
Cut 2.

Head
Cut 2.

Tail
Cut 2.

Fold

Head
Cut 1.

Saucy Mermaid, continued

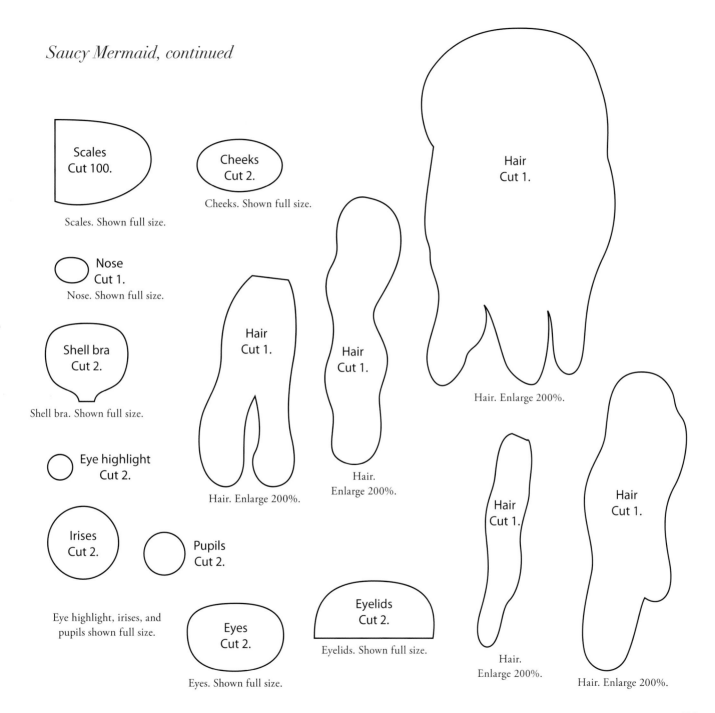

Scales
Cut 100.

Scales. Shown full size.

Cheeks
Cut 2.

Cheeks. Shown full size.

Hair
Cut 1.

Nose
Cut 1.

Nose. Shown full size.

Shell bra
Cut 2.

Shell bra. Shown full size.

Hair
Cut 1.

Hair
Cut 1.

Hair. Enlarge 200%.

Eye highlight
Cut 2.

Irises
Cut 2.

Pupils
Cut 2.

Eye highlight, irises, and
pupils shown full size.

Hair
Cut 1.

Hair. Enlarge 200%.

Hair.
Enlarge 200%.

Hair
Cut 1.

Hair
Cut 1.

Eyes
Cut 2.

Eyes. Shown full size.

Eyelids
Cut 2.

Eyelids. Shown full size.

Hair.
Enlarge 200%.

Hair. Enlarge 200%.

Starfish Appliqué Handbag

Project on page 66

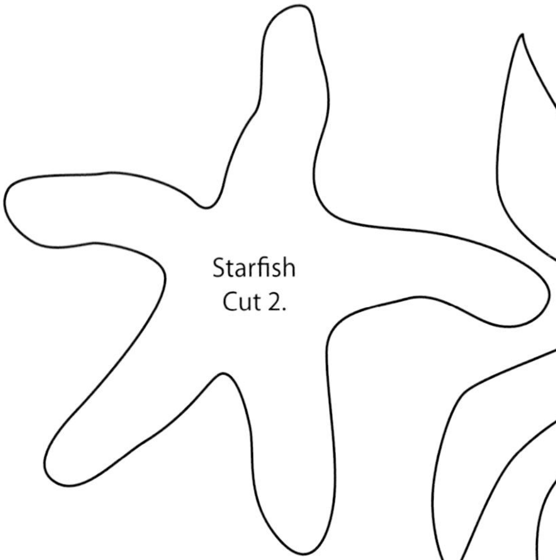

Starfish
Cut 2.

Starfish. Enlarge 200%.

Sand and Surf Bag

Project on page 82

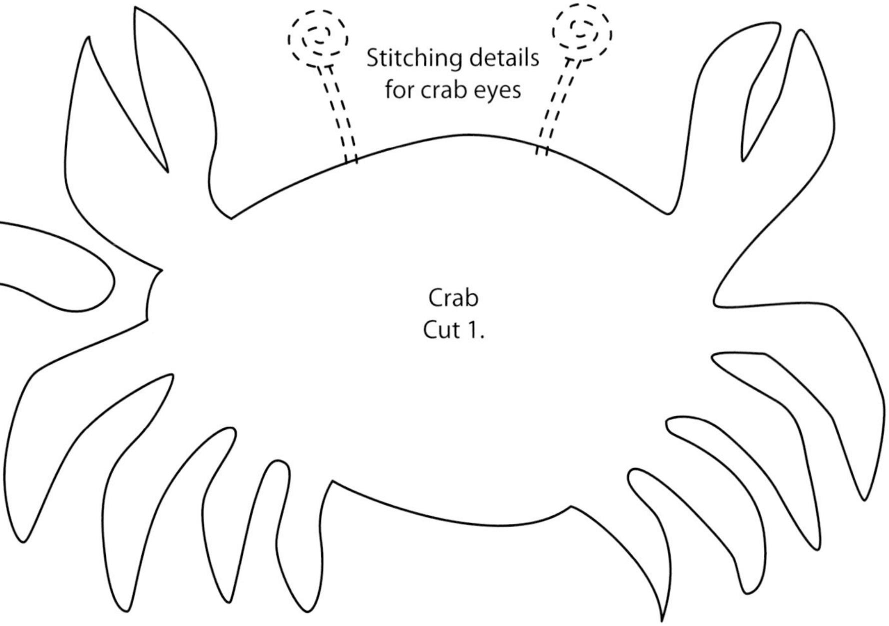

Stitching details
for crab eyes

Crab
Cut 1.

Hermit Crab Stuffie

Project on page 76

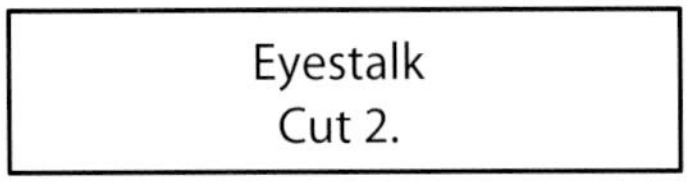

Eyestalk
Cut 2.

Eyestalk. Enlarge 200%.

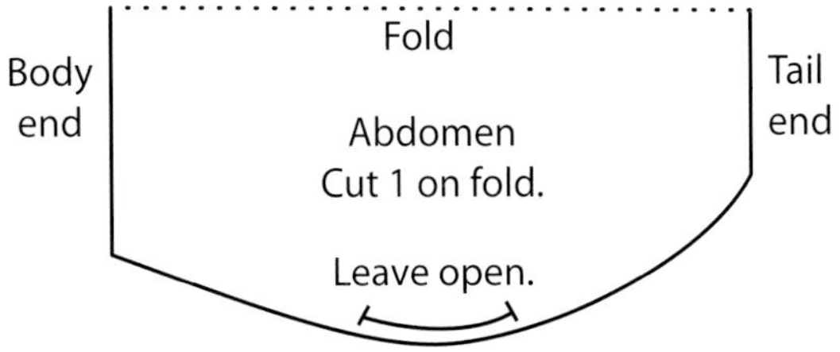

Body
end

Fold

Tail
end

Abdomen
Cut 1 on fold.

Leave open.

Abdomen. Enlarge 200%.

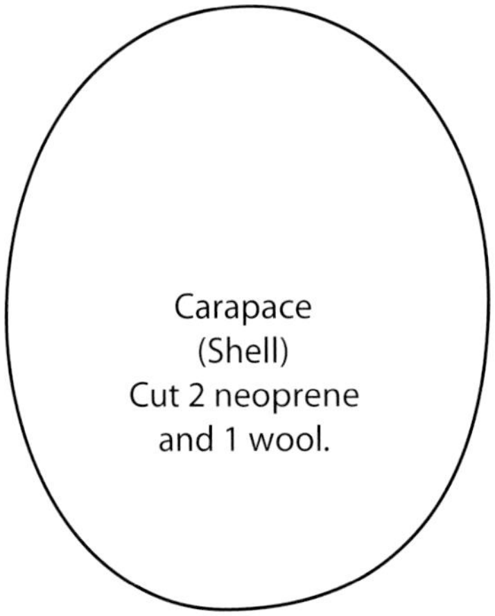

Carapace
(Shell)
Cut 2 neoprene
and 1 wool.

Carapace. Enlarge 200%.

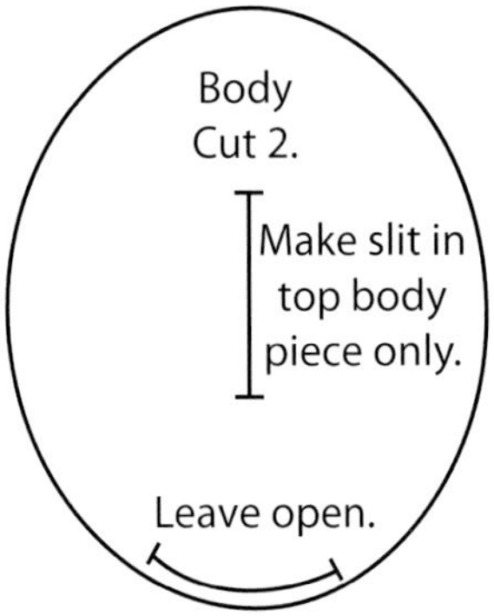

Body
Cut 2.

Make slit in
top body
piece only.

Leave open.

Body. Enlarge 200%.

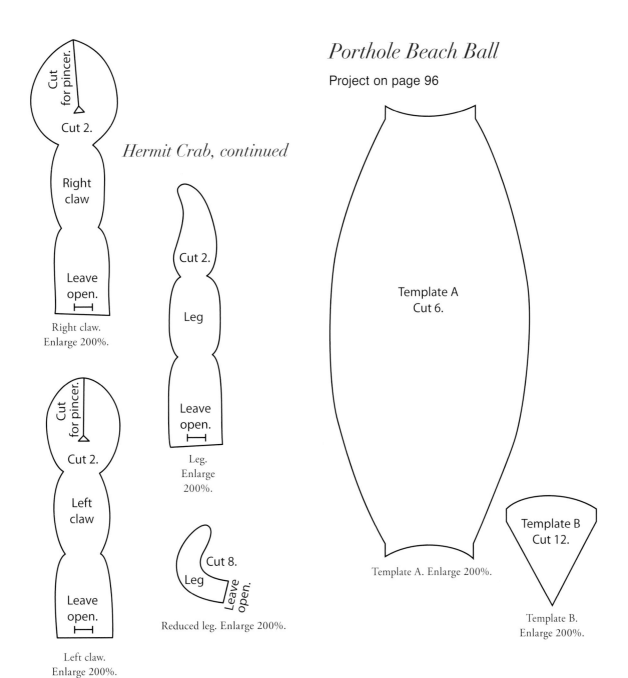

Cut
for pincer.

Cut 2.

Right
claw

Leave
open.

Right claw.
Enlarge 200%.

Hermit Crab, continued

Cut 2.

Leg

Leave
open.

Leg.
Enlarge
200%.

Cut
for pincer.

Cut 2.

Left
claw

Leave
open.

Left claw.
Enlarge 200%.

Cut 8.

Leg

Leave
open.

Reduced leg. Enlarge 200%.

Porthole Beach Ball

Project on page 96

Template A
Cut 6.

Template A. Enlarge 200%.

Template B
Cut 12.

Template B.
Enlarge 200%.

Beach Crab Pillow

Project on page 108

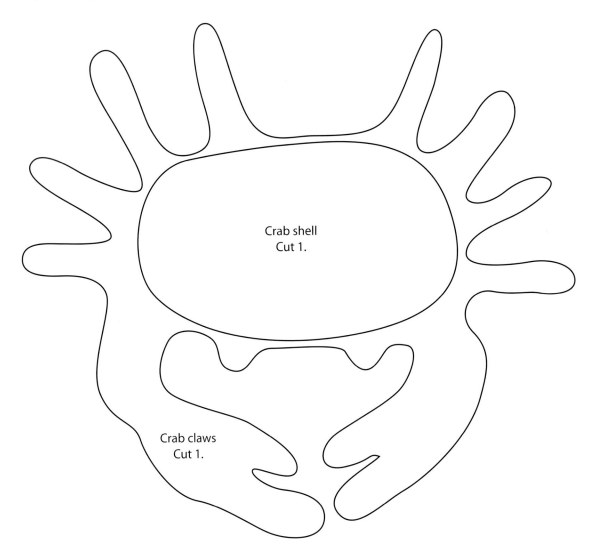

Crab shell
Cut 1.

Crab claws
Cut 1.

Embroidery Stitches

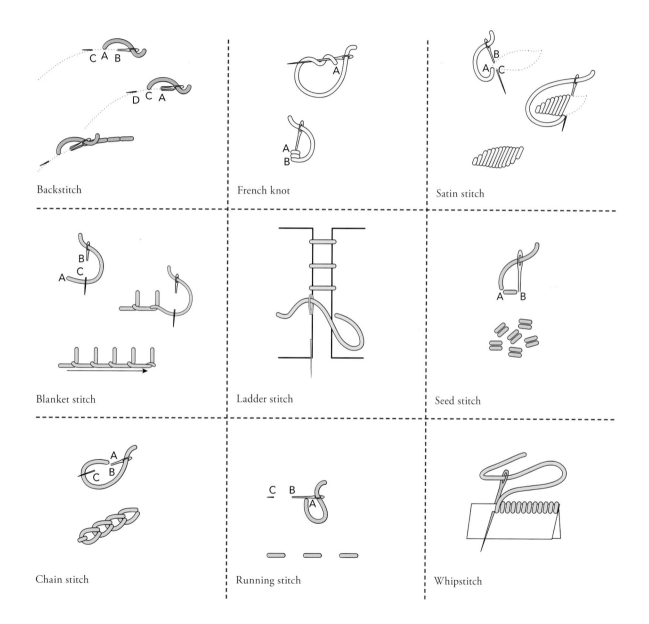

Backstitch

French knot

Satin stitch

Blanket stitch

Ladder stitch

Seed stitch

Chain stitch

Running stitch

Whipstitch

stashBOOKS

fabric arts for a handmade lifestyle

If you're craving beautiful authenticity in a time of mass-production...Stash Books is for you. Stash Books is a line of how-to books celebrating fabric arts for a handmade lifestyle. Backed by C&T Publishing's solid reputation for quality, Stash Books will inspire you with contemporary designs, clear and simple instructions, and engaging photography.

www.stashbooks.com